In His Glorious Name

The power and provision we have in the name of Jesus

And whatsoever ye shall ask in my name,
that will I do, that the Father
may be glorified in the Son
(John 14:13 KJV).

Daniel Gubitz

AXIOM PRESS

Mobile, Alabama

In His Glorious Name
by Daniel Gubitz

ISBN 978-1-58169-543-4
For Worldwide Distribution
Printed in the U.S.A.

Axiom Press
P.O. Box 191540 • Mobile, AL 36619
800-367-8203

Contents

Acknowledgments

A very special thank you to my wife, LaDonna, who knew this book was in me all the time and who supported me and pushed me as well as read and reread to be sure I got on paper what I was telling her was in my heart. When you look for a definition of wife, look for LaDonna. This lady has been my mainstay for forty-nine years. God just recently blessed us when He healed her of stage three, level C ovarian cancer, and, yes, we have the paperwork from MD Anderson Cancer Hospital in Houston, Texas, to prove it.

Even after all these blessings, He still allows me to call Him Father. Words cannot express the enjoyment I received from being allowed to write this book. Not only did God bless this phase of my life, but He has also blessed me throughout my life, though often I failed to see it. He has blessed me with two beautiful girls, Tanya and Andrea, and the three most wonderful grandchildren in the world, DJ, Viki, and Kaylee. What a blessing to see and hear these children loving and worshiping God.

Mike Jackson has been a minister all his life and a true friend of mine for most of it. His untiring support and insistence on me completing this book rises above the norm. Mike pastors New Life Assembly in Janesville, Wisconsin, a large and growing church full of loving and caring people. Without his time, wisdom, and true spiritual knowledge, I most probably would never have finished this work. Mike, thank you for being a friend at all levels.

This book was edited by Tina McCain, a lady God truly sent my way. Her commitment to God is well reflected in this work. I never knew the word *if* could cause so much trouble, let alone one little period. Tina has worked as the writing specialist in the

Jones Learning Center at the University of the Ozarks in Clarksville, Arkansas, for seventeen years. She thought those students gave her a challenge; I think I gave her a new appreciation for the incoming classes.

Introduction

This book came into being because my wife, LaDonna, was ill, and God's Word promises that whatsoever I ask in His name, I will receive. Trying to find the right name became a journey.

I was seeking God for Him to touch LaDonna and kept returning to John 14:13—ask in My name. Which name? I really wanted to reach the inner person of Jesus. I didn't want to pray a rubber stamp prayer. I really wanted to know I had talked to Jesus. I kept claiming the victory, but it seemed so shallow to just pray a prayer of healing. Again John 14:13 came into being, "Ask anything in my name," and as I read the Word of God it became abundantly clear that there is more than one name applied to Jesus. I wanted to find the name that would give me the results I was searching for, and that was healing for not only my wife, but my best friend for what will soon be the past fifty years.

I wanted to reach God's heart on her behalf. I wanted to know that He had made the decision pertaining to LaDonna's health.

I wanted to be able to tell my wife I had gotten her the best care as well as the best doctors and had spoken with the Greatest Healer there is, and that, of course, is God.

I didn't want to just tell her I had prayed and God would take care of it—don't worry. I wanted to be able to tell her I had heard from God and either He had a place waiting for her in heaven to put His arms around her and welcome her home, or that I was not sure what all He would lead her through but it was going to be okay. It was important for me to be able to tell her one or the other. I needed to hear from heaven.

How well I remember April 16, 2013 when her doctor came into the room and told us she was no longer in remission but was cancer free! Not only that, but he would no longer be seeing her because he only saw sick people. How cruel it would have been to have told her everything was going to be okay and that not have been the case.

What a glorious thought that we serve a living Lord whose name has no end! I am not naïve enough to think I have captured all His names, even though I attempted an exhaustive study. I am sure the Holy Spirit will continue to reveal the hidden mystery of His Word to others in His service.

It was never my intent, when all of this started, to write a book, or for that matter write anything. When I shared all the notes I had made, I was strongly encouraged to compile them and share them with others. Many of us, in crisis times, search for answers from many different people and sources. I trust God in some way this book will help in that search. If it helps just one person, then God has richly blessed me.

It seems the greatness and abilities of God the Father, God the Son, and God the Holy Spirit cannot be described in one word or, in fact, in many words. But knowing what your need is and knowing what salutation to give in your communication will certainly be more to the point in strengthening your faith and knowing and receiving according to God's will.

A dear friend of mine is the pastor of Christian Life Church in Austin, Texas. Rex Johnson not only is a dynamite preacher, but he also has a voice that, in my opinion, would bring rest to roses.

I heard him sing the song "I Can't Find the Words" and knew immediately that the words of the song explained what I was attempting to accomplish. Thank you, Tony Roberts, for giving me permission to include it in this book.

I Can't Find the Words
Tony Roberts

I've tried wonderful, marvelous, incredible, too,
Unbelievable, inconceivable, but these words would not do.
They all fell so short when I tried to convey
the greatness of Jesus
So I've just come to say:
I just can't find the words to really express,
The greatness of Jesus, so I must confess
I've tried big words and small words, but none that I've heard
Could describe Him. I just can't find the words.
I took down my dictionary,
I searched it all through.
I did a lot of looking in some other books, too.
But, when my search was over, I came right back around
To what I knew from the beginning:
No words could be found.
I just can't find the words to really express,
The greatness of Jesus, so I must confess
I've tried big words and small words, but none that I've heard
Could describe Him. I just can't find the words.
O, I'd like to describe Him, but I can't find the words.
Used by permission of Tony Roberts

Why is much made over the names of Jesus or God or the Holy Spirit? For all eternity, people have tried to explain the Trinity. In the Old Testament, God the Father is called many different names, all with varied meanings, yet none takes away from who He is; they just identify His many characteristics or attributes, if you will. In the New Testament, we learn Jesus was to be named Jesus (Matthew 1:21), and then we are told He was to be named Emmanuel (Matthew 1:23). He called Himself the Son of Man. So, obviously, a name has significance.

Many people have different abilities and are capable of meeting each of these abilities with great talent. There is no attempt to take away from one ability when calling upon another. If a person is a great painter as well as a great carpenter but you call upon that person to paint, you would expect that person to come prepared with the mindset and expectation of giving the best he or she has to offer as a painter. You would not want the person to show up with a hammer, saw, and other carpentry tools to paint. This is still the same person but with different abilities to accomplish your needs.

NAMES OF JESUS: A

Advocate

> *My dear children, I am writing this to you so that you will not sin. But if anyone does sin, we have an advocate who pleads our case before the Father. He is Jesus Christ, the one who is truly righteous* (1 John 2:1 NLT) .

We only have need of the best attorney when we know that we are guilty of something. When we are born, we are born guilty of sin. It is only natural that we would turn to Jesus for our defense. Who better to stand before God on our behalf and plead our case than the One who paid the supreme price by dying on the cross and taking on all our sins? Who better than the Righteous One, our Lord Jesus Christ? Jesus is our Advocate. Thus, He stands beside us to help us through anything and everything.

Our Advocate has the ability and willingness to help us through troubles, trials, confusion, discouragement, stress, loneliness, and hurt. There is nothing we can go through that this Advocate will not go through with us and then plead our case before God for all eternity.

Let's look at the credentials of this defense attorney (Advocate). He is the Son of God; He lived a sinless life on this earth. He is the Righteous One. He is in all ways perfect. Who else could enter into the presence of a perfect God except perfection itself? When Jesus the Advocate pleads our defense, it is not based on our reputation, our good works, our living a sinless life, or our having lived as good a life as we could. What is His pleading? His own righteousness.

As 1 John 2:1 says, "He is Jesus Christ, the One who is truly righteous."

• • • • •

All and in All

Where there is neither Greek nor Jew, circumcision nor uncircumcision, Barbarian, Scythian, bond nor free: but Christ is all, and in all (Colossians 3:11 KJV).

Truly, Jesus is All and in All. He is the One who, with God, created all things. He also is the One to whom all things will one day return. Jesus is our Savior, the One who will one day judge us. In the time between two events, creation and judgment, He is the One who preserves us.

Two things happen when we give our lives to Jesus. He enters into us, and we enter into Him. All believers are created equal. From this point, we either grow and mature or shrink and fall away. Jesus is all we need for salvation and unity with Him. As long as we allow Him to dwell in us, there will be no room for division or sin to enter.

Jesus is the bonding agent that brings all His followers together and makes them one in Him. He is our All and in All. We are no longer Jew and Gentile, no longer of this nation or that nation. No longer do we fit into any class other than that of being redeemed from sin by the precious blood of our Lord and Savior, Jesus.

Jesus should be the only tool by which we measure our lives. He should be all that matters as we move forward in service to Him.

As our All and in All, Jesus is never ashamed to call us His brothers or sisters, and the reason is that as believers we have set our lives apart from the world and have placed complete trust in Him. Sadly, some people cannot say as Paul did in Romans 1:16, "I am not ashamed of the gospel" (KJV). But this will all change once we make a sincere commitment to the All and in All, Jesus.

• • • • •

The Anchor for Our Souls

This hope is a strong and trustworthy anchor for our souls. It leads us through the curtain into God's inner sanctuary (Hebrews 6:19–20 NLT).

There are believers, there is faith, and there is Jesus. Faith is the rope that holds us to our Anchor, Jesus.

If a ship could sail without ever stopping, running into storms, or refueling, it would have no need for an anchor. But we, as ships upon the sea of life, do have to stop. Such things as jobs, families, and various other responsibilities and commitments cause us to stop. No one sails through life without running into the storms of temptation, troubles, trials, fears, doubts, worries, and sickness. When we are called upon to face the storms of death, there is no better anchor to be holding onto than the Anchor for Our Souls, the Lord Jesus Christ.

When we pause and think of all the unseen storms we have come through, not to mention all those that lie ahead should Jesus delay His return, we can only give thanks for the past and keep our faith tied to the Anchor for Our Souls, Jesus, for the future.

Jesus puts stability into our lives when we allow Him to serve as our Anchor. When we give control of our lives to Him but then take it back and try to serve as our own anchor, this double mindedness causes waves of unstableness. We get confused and tossed every which way.

No matter how torn the sail, how battered the boat, or how badly damaged the rudder, our Anchor, the Lord Jesus Christ, will keep us from being destroyed or lost on the sea of life. We need to anchor our eyes, ears, voice, and actions on the Anchor for Our Souls, Jesus. No anchor, no Jesus, no hope!

Author of Eternal Salvation

And being made perfect, he became the author of eternal salvation unto all them that obey him (Hebrews 5:9 KJV).

When we think of someone being an author, we think of someone with an idea of a plot and an ending. In most cases, authors like to have happy endings. Certainly those of us who follow Jesus and obey His teachings know the happy ending He has for us. We notice that because He is the Author of Eternal Salvation; this ending is forever.

Jesus lived as an example for us, died as an example for us, and rose from the dead as an example for us. He became the source as well as the Author of Eternal Salvation. We hear a lot about salvation. We are told that Jesus is the One who gives salvation and that God offers it to us. We are told we should want it, but what is it?

Salvation is like a judge declaring us not guilty because

someone else is paying for our guilt. We are being offered something we didn't work to get. We cannot and did not pay anything for our salvation. This gift will change the direction of our lives for all eternity. Our hope will be renewed, and our outlook on life will be changed forever. Peace will be the ruling factor in our lives. A smile will be the beginning of each day.

When we obey Jesus and follow His teachings, righteousness forgives us. It will carry us successfully through all temptations and trials of this life and allow us to spend all eternity with the source and Author of Eternal Salvation.

At times, doubts and fears that perhaps we messed up and will miss eternity with Jesus may start to slip into our thoughts. Remember, we are not serving the temporary author. We are not serving the partial author. We are not serving an unfinished author. We are serving the eternal Author, Jesus.

NAMES OF JESUS: B

Babe

And this shall be a sign unto you; Ye shall find the babe wrapped in swaddling clothes, lying in a manger (Luke 2:12 KJV).

Notice that the shepherds didn't ask for any signs, but they received one. Apparently, the angels expected the shepherds to start searching right away for this Babe, so they gave them a description of what to look for. Finding the Babe, and more importantly the right Babe, would be the proof of the truth of the angel's word down to the smallest detail. Many babies could have been born in Bethlehem, but how many would be born in a manger?

Several things are revealed regarding the birth of this Babe. First, our Savior was fully human. Born in the flesh just like you and me, Jesus came as truly man as well as truly God.

Second, He was simply a man: "Ye shall find the babe," as just a babe. Very little can be said about Him. There was nothing special as far as the Babe being from royalty or being born into a family recognized for its wealth or its special contribution to the local area. He, quite simply, was just a Babe.

Third, we notice Jesus came as a loving person first to win the hearts of His parents and then to continue on to win the hearts of humankind. Fourth, for the most part, He was rejected. The custom in the East at the time of Jesus' birth was to dress the very young in folds of linen and woolen. But the dressing of the Babe would seem to indicate that not a lot of preparation and planning went into His birth.

It would seem then as now that the world was not ready for our Lord and Savior, Jesus Christ.

* * * * *

The Beginning of the Creation

> *And unto the angel of the church of the Laodiceans write; These things saith the Amen, the faithful and true witness, the beginning of the creation of God* (Revelation 3:14 KJV).

Here we see Jesus as the Head or Governor or King, if you will, of all creation. We also see Him here as the Maker, Provider, and Protector of His creation. These roles would apply to all things in heaven as well as on earth, visible as well as invisible.

In the area of astronomy, Jesus is called the Star and the Sun. In the area of zoology, Jesus is called the Lamb of God and the Lion of Judah. In the area of biology, He is called the Tree of Life. In the area of botany, He is called the Rose of Sharon and the Lily of the Valleys. In the area of geology, He is called the Rock of Ages as well as the Cornerstone. In the area of mineralogy, He is compared to sardius and jasper stones. In the area of philology, Jesus is called Alpha and Omega. This would make Jesus the sole source of all good things in all phases of life—wealth, love, peace, direction, and dependence.

Anything that will ever have any real meaning or significance in our lives starts from that point. Regardless of age or position in life, we can trace all good things back to the moment of our creation in Jesus.

In the beginning when Jesus called all things into order and created a purpose for all things, He gave directions as well as wisdom and a freedom to choose. Jesus continues to do the very same today.

Just as the beginning of creation was done as an act of free will and love and a desire to fellowship with humankind, it continues today for the same reason. Reach out and hold to the unchanging hand of the Beginning of the Creation of God, Jesus.

• • • • •

Bishop of Your Souls (The Guardian of Your Souls)

For ye were as sheep going astray; but are now returned unto the Shepherd and Bishop of your souls (1 Peter 2:25 KJV).

Once you were like sheep who wandered away. But now you have turned to your Shepherd, the Guardian of your souls (1 Peter 2:25 NLT).

The word *Bishop* has several meanings, such as protector, caretaker, guide, guardian, overseer, or director. What a beautiful verbal picture of Jesus watching over our souls! When we surrender our lives to Him, He takes complete charge of them.

Why do we need a Guardian for our souls? The answer is quite simple. When we are left on our own, we become vulnerable. Just think back to the Garden of Eden. The influence of God was everywhere. The ability to speak face-to-face with Him and walk in His presence was a daily routine as well as a daily choice. However, even with God's presence, we know what decision was made as we now live with the results of that choice.

Who else but Jesus would be qualified to protect and provide for our souls? When our souls are troubled or seem to be at a crossroads of a difficult decision, when we are trying to make bright futures for ourselves and have no idea what lies in store for us, we should want no one other than Jesus to be the One who is guarding our souls.

When we trust our souls to Jesus and are obedient to Him as the Guardian of our souls, He will not only meet our souls' needs but will provide for our souls' wants as well.

Part of Jesus guarding our souls includes His willingness to forgive us as we sometimes stray from His leading; He restores us to His protection and continues to guard our souls.

There is not a soul who is not dear to Jesus. He was, is, and always will be the supreme Bishop and Protector of His Church and our souls.

• • • • •

The Breaker

The Breaker [the Messiah] will go up before them. They will break through, pass in through the gate and go out through it, and their King will pass on before them, the Lord at their head (Micah 2:13 AMP).

Isn't this a great name for Jesus? How do we compile a list of all the things Jesus breaks down for us? It seems the list gets something new added to it every day.

The great thing about Jesus is that He doesn't break things in our lives and leave them shattered and scattered. He rebuilds our lives so that sin cannot gain victory over us and death can't keep us from Him.

It wasn't until Jesus came to earth, died on the cross, and rose from the dead that humankind had any hope of putting sin out of their lives. When Jesus took control of death, He opened the door that blocked our ability to approach God. Because Jesus did this, we not only have direct access to God but also an ongoing relationship with the precious Holy Spirit.

In Jesus the Breaker, we must recognize that nothing and no one else had, has, or ever will have power over sin. He also broke down the destruction between Jew and Gentile.

He not only broke the fear, but He forever removed the fear of our spending a lifetime separated from God. Jesus has broken or is willing to break the pride that we too often carry; some may call it self-righteousness.

If Jesus isn't the Breaker in our lives, He stands ready to become so if we will just ask Him. All pain, hurt, sorrow, disappointments, and fears that are brought on by not serving God can be broken down by Jesus the Breaker. Simply ask Him.

NAMES OF JESUS: C

Chief Shepherd

And when the chief Shepherd shall appear, ye shall receive a crown of glory that fadeth not away (1 Peter 5:4 KJV).

There are many shepherds in Christianity today. Many are leading in the direction that Jesus established, but some are leading in a self-serving direction. Some are leading in a confused direction. However, there is only one Chief Shepherd, and all other shepherds are subject to His direction and judgments regardless of the direction they choose.

Jesus as the Shepherd is classed in at least four different shepherd roles.

In the book of John and in the Psalms, He is referred to as the *Good Shepherd.* He is willing not only to risk His life but also to lose it for His sheep.

In Hebrews, He is called the *Great Shepherd.* He left the tomb having gained victory over death, and now He perfects His sheep.

In 1 Peter, He is called the *Shepherd and Bishop of Your Souls*. He is called this because He stands ready and has full authority to welcome back any of His sheep who have wandered off and gone astray.

And in 1 Peter, He is also called the *Chief Shepherd* because one day He will return to earth in all His glory and greatness. His appearance will be to reward His faithful followers.

Christ of God

He said unto them, But whom say ye that I am? Peter answering said, The Christ of God (Luke 9:20 KJV).

Peter is saying that Jesus is the Anointed One of God, the Messiah and the Deliver, as well as the long-awaited Savior. Jesus is the complete fulfillment of all the prophecies pertaining to the coming of the Messiah.

Jesus' mission was that of saving humankind, a premeditated, deliberate, singleness of mind that only Jesus could fulfill.

While Peter did not understand a lot, he knew for certain that Jesus was the Messiah, the Christ, and the Son of God. Peter knew this before the cross, the resurrection, and the ascension. Perhaps he did not grasp the exact course of Jesus' ministry, yet he knew who Jesus was.

Jesus was not only sent by God on a deliberate and purposeful mission but was also qualified to fulfill it.

We rest our lives on what we think about Jesus. Whether we reject or accept Him, we must understand that Jesus is the Son of God made flesh who died on the cross for our sins, was raised from the dead, and now sits at the right hand of God.

The single most important question we will ever be asked is who we think Christ is. The answer is as important as the question. This is not a question anyone else can answer for us, and no one can escape being asked and having to answer.

Who do you say Jesus is? Many have answered a prophet, a wise man, a good man, a great religious leader, a representative of truth, goodness, and love. While all of these are true, only one answer will forgive us of our sins and create a new life for us. That answer is Jesus is the Christ, the living Son of God.

Counselor

For a child has been born for us, a son given to us; authority rests upon his shoulders; and he is named Wonderful Counselor, Mighty God, Everlasting Father, Prince of Peace (Isaiah 9:6 NRSV).

While many can attend school and obtain a degree in counseling, nothing compares to real life experience. Jesus lived as a man and was flesh and blood just as you and I. He suffered unbelievable pain and was put to a cruel death. He experienced rejection and ridicule. He was laughed at, made fun of, bullied, lied about, and falsely accused. He suffered every kind of pain imaginable and was tempted in every way we can think of, yet He still showed us how to love through these experiences and come out a better person for experiencing it all.

His mother was not married (Matthew 1:18–19). He was born in horrible conditions (Luke 2:7). His parents were poor (Luke 2:24). As a baby, His life was threatened (Matthew 2:13). He was the cause of unimaginable sorrow (Matthew 2:16). As a baby, He was moved around a lot (Matthew 2:13). He was brought up in a horrible place (Luke 2:39). His father probably died during His youth (Luke 6:3). He had to support His family (Matthew 13:53–58). He had no home, not even a place to lay His head (Matthew 8:20; Luke 9:58).

The religionists opposed and hated Him (Mark 14:1–2). He was accused of being insane (Mark 3:21). He was accused of being demon possessed (Mark 3:22). His own family opposed Him (Mark 3:31–32). He was hated, rejected, and opposed by those He spoke to (Matthew 13:53–58; Luke 4:28–29). His close friend betrayed Him (Mark 14:10–11, 18). He was rejected, deserted, and forsaken by all His friends (Mark 14:50).

He was tried by the high court of the land on charges of treason (John 18:33).

The trials Jesus went through for us could never be taught in a classroom. Because He has felt what we are feeling, we can depend on Him without fail to hold our hands and hearts, to walk with us through any difficulties in life itself, and then to walk with us through all eternity. Jesus truly is the Counselor.

• • • • •

Creator

> *Christ himself is the Creator who made everything in heaven and earth, the things we can see and the things we can't; the spirit world with its kings and kingdoms, its rulers and authorities; all were made by Christ for his own use and glory* (Colossians 1:16 TLB).

Nothing in the past, present, or future has, does, or will exist that Christ has not created. If other planets exist with life on them, if other dimensions or invisible worlds exist, or if powers, principalities, thrones, or dominions exist, they really do not matter because He created them.

Creation took place in His very being. The world was created by His word. He desired the world within His heart. The world was planned by the mind of Christ; it was destined by His will. Within Jesus, the world was born. The love that was in His heart moved Him to creation. The richness of His grace compelled Him to will the world. The world came into being by the awesome power of His spoken word.

Christ created all things, doing away with any notion that He is created. He made everything out of nothing, not just creation as a whole but every single detail, element, and being, angelic, human, or spirit.

The world and all in it, on it, above it, or below it were created by and belong to Him. He cares for His creation. The problems of the world are not due to His attitude toward the world but because of sin and the attitude of humankind.

The answer to the world's problems is not to be found in humankind's ability. The answer is to be found in humankind giving their hearts, minds, and lives back to the Creator, the Lord Jesus Christ.

NAMES OF JESUS: D

Door

"I am the door: by me if any man enter in, he shall be saved, and shall go in and out, and find pasture" (John 10:9 KJV).

No other door leads to salvation. Jesus is the only Door that leads to security and peace. He leads us into living waters and spiritual nourishment. No other door leads to not only abundant but eternal life. Anyone who offers another door is a liar and a thief, and those who use that door and accept those lies walk through a door of destruction and eternal damnation.

A door implies some type of action on our part to open or close. We have the opportunity to open the door to Jesus now. Many things can keep us from opening the door—our own unrighteousness, our own self-righteousness, laziness, death, and, of course, the return of Jesus.

It was God who shut the door on the ark, and nothing or no one else could open it. No matter what prayers or wealth was offered, the door was shut.

We still have the opportunity to commit our lives to Jesus and serve Him now and for all eternity. The real beauty in serving Jesus is that we get to make the choice, and He will respect that choice for all eternity.

When the Door, Jesus, is opened, everything about Jesus—all His grace, all His goodness, all His healing, all His provisions, all His wisdom, all His knowledge, all His understanding, all His insight, the totality of Jesus—is opened unto us. All we have to do is open our hearts to the open Door, Jesus.

NAMES OF JESUS: E

Everlasting Strength

Trust ye in the Lord for ever: for in the Lord Jehovah is everlasting strength (Isaiah 26:4 KJV).

Jesus has all power to bring to pass all that He has promised. When we are given a direction and a job to complete by Jesus, we do it and complete it by His strength. We can keep the strength to do His work by keeping in touch with Him through prayer. When we are obedient to Him, we can see lives changed, hearts touched, and souls won to the kingdom. Widows and orphans are cared for, and the less fortunate are fed and clothed. All of this is done through the strength of Jesus.

God keeps His word. He is unchanging; therefore, we need His strength in order to do His work. With Jesus' strength, we will be honest and consistent in our words and actions. Lying is a weakness and the beginning of most all of our problems; whether we lie to Jesus or to another person, it comes from our weakness. Since Jesus has all power on earth and in heaven, He has no need to lie to accomplish His will. When Jesus is given control of our lives, we have His strength, so we have no need to lie either.

We seem to get ourselves in real trouble when we try to do things in our own strength. We make decisions regardless of how important they may be without praying and seeking God's direction. We make decisions that go against the principles of the Bible, God's Holy Word.

We often fail to wait on the Lord for direction and make quick decisions that get us ahead of Jesus. Or we too often sit back and wait when Jesus is trying to move us forward. That is why it is critical to stay in constant communication with Him through prayer and reading and studying His precious Holy Word. Jesus, His Word, and everything about Him are unchanging and everlasting. What a privilege we have to draw on Him, Everlasting Strength.

NAMES OF JESUS: F

Faith

But before faith came, we were kept under the law, shut up unto the faith which should afterwards be revealed (Galatians 3:23 KJV).

The Living Bible states in Galatians 3:23, "Until Christ came." When Jesus came, we were able to understand what we needed to believe in. We were also able to understand what it was we were to believe as well us why we should believe it. Simply put, Jesus is Faith—Faith is Jesus.

The Old Testament believers were justified in their faith by trusting in God's grace. They didn't know much about God's plan. Their faith was in what would be revealed, and that revelation was Jesus.

Before Jesus, we were under the law. With Jesus, there is not a list of do's and don'ts. We no longer struggle with someone making animal sacrifices on our behalf. Jesus took care of all of this by sacrificing Himself once and for all. We are totally free from all ceremonial law and influence of humankind.

The promises of God do not come through the law but rather through the righteousness of Faith, Jesus.

We will not spend eternity with Jesus because we were moral or joined the church and were baptized. Doing good deeds or good works, trying to keep the Ten Commandments, or considering ourselves religious will not cause us to gain eternity with Jesus. We will spend eternity with Jesus because we believe in Him, and God counts Jesus as our Righteousness.

When Jesus walked as a man on this earth, He took our sins

upon Himself and died on the cross for the sin for which, in reality, we should have died.

When we totally and completely accept and trust Jesus for who He is and what He has done for us, then and only then do we start to understand Faith.

• • • • •

Faithful and True

Then I saw heaven opened, and a white horse was standing there. Its rider was named Faithful and True, for he judges fairly and wages a righteous war (Revelation 19:11 NLT).

What a great name! Just think, we not only serve but are also friends with someone who is Faithful and True.

Jesus is Faithful in that all of His promises will be kept; He is True in completing everything He starts. Jesus came to earth to start preparations for us to join Him in heaven and left to sit at the right hand of His Father, God, to complete that very thing. What a contrast to the world where lies and deceitfulness are as common as faithfulness and truth are uncommon!

We become faithful and true by following Jesus' example. He showed Himself Faithful and True by coming from His home in heaven. He is the only eternal truth we will ever know. We become faithful and true when we accept Jesus for who He is.

There is no deity in manmade metal, woodcarvings, or concrete figures. There is, however, an abundance of deity in the living Son of the Living God, and He is with us wherever we go. He is Faithful and True.

When we examine Jesus as being Faithful and True, we see

Him as being Faithful to His Father, God, and to witnessing about Him. Jesus is a fountain of truth; He cannot lie. Not only is Jesus perfect, but He is perfectly honest. Jesus is also completely honest in that He does not leave us wondering about what the results of our actions will be. Everything God wanted done or said, Jesus did, and He did it completely and perfectly. Not only are Jesus' words and examples Faithful and True, but His past, present, and future are the same.

Jesus, was, is, and always will be Faithful and True.

Faithful Witness

And from Jesus Christ, who is the faithful witness, and the first begotten of the dead, and the prince of the kings of the earth. Unto him that loved us, and washed us from our sins in his own blood (Revelation 1:5 KJV).

Here we see Jesus in all His sovereignty. The Faithful Witness, His words are directly from God. Jesus came to us from heaven, and His sole purpose is to witness to us about God the Father. Everything Jesus said is proven to be factual. Through His life, His death, and His resurrection, He revealed and lived the truth in all ways. He taught us what He heard from God. He showed in His miracles what He taught. Even near death, He refused to deny God and His teachings. He was and is the Faithful Witness.

Both believers and Jesus are called witnesses. However, many believers are afraid to witness to others because they don't feel that the change they experienced was glamorous or their testimony electrifying, so they just sit back and say and do nothing. But we fail and fail miserably when we think we have done something for Jesus. Remember, Jesus did it all. He paid the debt before we ever got the bill.

Jesus has never told a single lie. He wants us to know God. Jesus has all knowledge concerning what He spoke about. Since Jesus is perfect, He has no reason to misrepresent the truth, to deceive, or to fear evil, and He has nothing to gain. He is truth.

• • • • •

Flesh and Blood

> *Forasmuch then as the children are partakers of flesh and blood, he also himself likewise took part of the same; that through death he might destroy him that had the power of death, that is, the devil* (Hebrews 2:14 KJV).

If you want to know what real grace is, look at Jesus. He bodily took on our being and our nature and became like us. We had no say in our birth. Jesus chose ("took part") to become flesh and blood.

Because of Jesus' love for us, He made human nature part of His divine nature. To gain forgiveness for us and to fully understand the pains, thoughts, temptations, and desires we experience, He experienced the human side of life. When we talk to Jesus, we are talking to someone who has been where we are. Regardless of how desperate we might think our situation, Jesus has been there. When He intercedes on our behalf, He knows exactly what He is talking about.'

By becoming flesh and blood, He could die and be raised

from the dead for our benefit. He was able to conquer death and take full control of it. We no longer have to live in fear of death and dying.

When we know we belong to Jesus, we know death is the door that opens into eternal life with Jesus.

Friend

Jesus said, "My friend, go ahead and do what you have come for." Then the others grabbed Jesus and arrested him (Matthew 26:50 NLT).

Once Jesus becomes our Friend, He never stops being one. When Jesus called Judas "friend," it was said as an act of love; it definitely was not sarcasm.

In order for us to be a friend of Jesus, we have to know Him as much as He knows us. We have to know what His teachings are, what His beliefs are, what He loves, and what He hates. We have to know what motivates Him, what causes Him pain and discomfort, what will draw Him close to us, and what will push Him away.

Being a friend of Jesus is both active and positive. It is cheerful as well as intimate; it is honorable as well as valuable. Perhaps the greatest thing about this friendship is that it is personal, very personal. Jesus is a friend to each individual's needs; it is not a friendship of one-size-fits-all.

What kind of friendship do you have with Jesus? When you approach Him, is it as a servant or as someone you know intimately? Do you know what He expects from you as well as what you expect from Him out of your friendship? Do you love Him as much as you want Him to love you?

The great thing about a friendship with Jesus is that you can know as much about Him as He knows about you, and that, my friend, is everything! Jesus truly is a Friend. He wants to be our Friend to the point that He died so He could be.

If you want or need a friend who will stay closer than a brother, then just call on Jesus, our Friend!

• • • • •

Friend of Sinners

"The Son of Man, on the other hand, feasts and drinks, and you say, 'He's a glutton and a drunkard, and a friend of tax collectors and other sinners!' But wisdom is shown to be right by its results" (Matthew 11:19 NLT).

How blessed we are that Jesus came to save us sinners. While on earth, He associated with some of the worst in society. He ate with them, walked and talked with them, made Himself available to them, and attended social functions with them. But He did not do so for the same reasons you or I might do those things. Jesus' sole purpose was to reach those in need of forgiveness and salvation, not to be a part of the worldly group.

We should be thankful that Jesus did associate with sinners because if He hadn't, we would be condemned to a life of eternal separation from Him. Isn't it great that we can call the Creator of all things, including life, our Friend? Not only is He our Friend, but we know for a fact that He is the greatest example of what a friend should be—always caring about us, loving us, and forgiving us. He never puts us down for our past deeds. When we walk away from Him, deny we ever knew Him, and hurt Him in unimaginable ways, He still stands with open arms welcoming us back. He moves forward with us as though we had never deserted Him. We will never find another Friend like Jesus.

• • • • •

Fullness of God

> *For in Christ lives all the fullness of God in a human body* (Colossians 2:9 NLT).

This verse tells us that Jesus and God are in fact two separate deities, but God manifested all His deity in Jesus. Jesus is no less than God. In a perfect and absolute sense, Jesus is God.

By Jesus being the Fullness of God, we know that not a single part of God's nature is missing from Jesus. Just as God the Father has the full nature and being of God, so Jesus has the same nature and being of God—before He came to earth, while He was upon this earth, and with Him as He sits at the right hand of God the Father. This was not a temporary gift.

When we receive Jesus in our lives, we receive this fullness. We receive wisdom, redemption, righteousness, and sanctification: wisdom to understand God and fill the purpose He has for our lives; redemption so that we may spend eternity with Him; righteousness so that we can see and know sin both in our lives as well as in the world; and sanctification so that we can live for and with Him and serve Him with willing and obedient hearts.

NAMES OF JESUS: G

Galilean

"Oh, is he a Galilean?" Pilate asked (Luke 23:6 NLT).

We can call Jesus what we want, but that does not change who He is. Pilate knew Jesus was innocent, but Pilate wanted to please the crowd. So when he heard the word *Galilee*, it was his way out. Pilate wanted to avoid doing what was right; his only thought was of himself. He wanted the Jews to handle the situation themselves. He turned Jesus over to Herod as a way to avoid having to make a decision on what to do with Jesus.

How often do we look to please the crowd and not do what is right? How many times does Jesus show up in our lives, and we try to pass Him off as something else? How often do we feel tugging at our hearts and know that it is Jesus wanting to come in? We are faced every day with the same question—what will I do with Jesus? While this may be a simple question, the answer will be honored for all eternity.

Gift of God

Thank God for this gift too wonderful for words! (2 Corinthians 9:15 NLT).

There has never been a gift given by God or humankind greater than Jesus. He is the supreme Gift of God. When we think of His love and compassion, all that is gained by serving Him, and all the suffering He went through for us, no words can describe this Gift. How do we explain this Gift that brought humankind out of darkness and into His blessed light? This Gift reached down and pulled humankind's soul from the hand of Satan and placed it into the hand of God.

What a blessing when we take time to really think through what Jesus has done, is doing, and will continue to do. We should want to share this Gift with others as well as spend considerable time thanking God for His Gift. When we take time to sincerely thank someone for a gift that we really appreciate, it puts both the giver and the receiver into the same frame of mind, one of gratitude, love, and sincerity. Maybe it is time to stop and reflect on everything in our lives that God has provided or protected us from. If we really made a list of all the answered prayers in our lives and all He has provided without our asking, how many pages would it fill?

Can we even remember all His answered prayers in our lifetime, especially those that seemed like a matter of life or death or those that seemed as if we would surely lose everything if they were not answered? Have we ever taken the time to thank Him for those gifts of answered prayers? Do we spend as much time thanking Him, with the same zeal and seriousness, as we do asking Him in the first place? How can we not when we have received such a gift as Jesus?

God's Mysterious Plan

I want them to be encouraged and knit together by strong ties of love. I want them to have complete confidence that they understand God's mysterious plan, which is Christ himself (Colossians 2:2 NLT).

To many people, God is a mystery. He shouldn't be because He stands ready through the anointing power of the Holy Spirit and the saving power of His Son the Lord Jesus Christ to make Himself personally known to us.

In the Scriptures, a mystery is not like a whodunit in a television show or some well-written novel. In the Scriptures, a mystery means that God is, for the first time, revealing something of which we had no knowledge. It cannot be discovered by humankind because it is a revelation from God. What is the mystery? Jesus!

Through Jesus, one finds all the answers to the mysteries of whether God really exists, really cares about us, is really concerned about our daily lives, and if we can really know Him personally, be free from the fear of death, and if there is really such a thing as life after death. All the answers to these mysteries and many more have been answered by one Person, and that Person is Jesus—God's Mysterious Plan.

God's Son

The beginning of the gospel of Jesus Christ, the Son of God (Mark 1:1 KJV).

Jesus Christ is His official title; Son of God is His personal title. Notice that Jesus is the Son, not a son of God. Jesus is the only Son, the only begotten Son of God. Throughout the New Testament, the writers claim that Jesus is the Son of God.

Jesus was fully man and fully divine, and in this unique relationship, He depended on and obeyed His Father. At Jesus' baptism, God Himself authenticated Jesus as His Son, and John the Baptist was a witness to it.

Jesus was truth. One truth was that God sent Him into the world as flesh and blood. Just like any other person, He had the nature of a human; and since He did, He experienced all the trials, temptations, and suffering that we experience. He went through what we go through; therefore, He is able to understand and guide us through all the trials of life if we will just let Him.

Another truth about Jesus is that He is the Son of God. He was the Son of God before He came to earth; He was the Son of God while He was upon the earth, and He now sits at the right hand of God the Father as the Son of God. His life on earth proved that He was the Son of God. He lived on earth and never sinned. His resurrection proved He is the Son of God. All others who have died are buried and gone. None have been seen since. Not Jesus. He died, was buried, arose, walked on this earth again, and now lives in the presence of His Father.

We know that Jesus' death on the cross brought forgiveness for our sins and that Jesus is not a mere human being. Jesus is deity, not one among many but God Himself in the flesh. Once Jesus comes into our lives, there is no doubt that Jesus is God's Son.

God's Ultimate Yes

For Jesus Christ, the Son of God, does not waver between "Yes" and "No." He is the one whom Silas, Timothy, and I preached to you, and as God's ultimate "Yes," he always does what he says (2 Corinthians 1:19 NLT).

Why is this name so very important to us? Perhaps one of the main reasons is that it sums up God's position on all of His promises to us. Think of His promises of peace, forgiveness, healing, joy, salvation, eternal life, blessings, and many more as "Yes." They are all available to us if we live a "Yes" life with Him. Yes, I will be obedient to Him and His Word. Yes, I will keep Him first in all phases of my life, including, prayer, fasting, tithing, serving, and witnessing to and for Him.

Jesus lived a "Yes" life in that He fulfilled all the promises of God. First Peter 3:18 tells us that He never sinned. He was faithful and obedient in that He died for us (Hebrews 2:9). To this day He continually intercedes for those of us who follow and serve Him (Romans 8:34). God promised that He would send a Savior, and He did by sending Jesus. In turn, Jesus said yes to the Father by living a life of examples for us to follow.

If we were to look for a guarantee or warranty pertaining to the promises of God that are placed throughout the Bible (there are many, and it would do us all good to search them out and study them), we would find that by Jesus' birth, His ministry of miracles, His death on the cross, and His resurrection, we have this guarantee.

We find in searching God's Word that all the promises of God come through Jesus. Therefore, no promise from God can ever fail.

In Jesus, we see the "Yes" of God's heart. If we say yes to

Jesus coming into our hearts and lives, then Jesus is saying yes to our lives for all the promises of God. All of this is because of Jesus, God's Ultimate Yes.

• • • • •

The Guarantee of a Better Covenant

Because of this oath, Jesus has become the guarantee of a better covenant (Hebrews 7:22 NIV).

When you research the word *guarantee*, in most instances, the definitions of the word describe Jesus. For example, we find the following definitions: something that assures a particular outcome; a promise or an assurance; one person assumes responsibility for paying another's debts or fulfilling another's responsibilities; to assume responsibility for the quality or performance; to make certain; to answer for the debt; something that makes a specified condition or outcome certain; to undertake to protect or keep secure, as against injury, loss; a payment given as a guarantee that an obligation will be met; an assurance of help when needed. Have we ever thought of Jesus being all these things? He is and so much more.

What does Jesus guarantee pertaining to this better covenant, and for whom does He guarantee it? He guarantees it for the poor who have little hope of ever having anything, for the rich who have little hope of ever enjoying anything, for the dying (which includes all of us except those who are living at His return), for all who are in some way afflicted in this world, but especially for those who face Satan's temptations and trials and have decided to live for Jesus.

Compare the first covenant, which had conditions and could fail, to Jesus, who is unconditional in His love for us and will never fail us. The first covenant was temporary and never meant to last. Jesus, who is the Guarantee, will last for all eternity. According to Hebrews 8:7–9, the first covenant had flaws. Jesus was, is, and always will be flawless. He is the epitome of perfection.

Jesus made it possible to go directly to God. If we accept the fact that Jesus sacrificed Himself on the cross for our sins, then God will forgive us our sins and create in us a new person. All of this is because of Jesus, the Guarantee of a Better Covenant.

NAMES OF JESUS: H

He Who Sanctifies

For both he that sanctifieth and they who are sanctified are all of one: for which cause he is not ashamed to call them brethren (Hebrews 2:11 KJV).

When we ask Jesus into our lives and receive forgiveness of our sins, we are said to be sanctified. As we grow in the Lord with the help of the Holy Spirit, we are said to be growing in sanctification.

Two things are required to receive sanctification. One is *separation*. We must start on the road of separating ourselves from the ways of sin as well as from the places of sin and sin's habits. The other thing that is required to receive sanctification is *renovation*. We must strive to rebuild our lives. We need to start praying, reading God's Word, and putting Him first in our lives.

Two agents are involved in the process of sanctification. One is He Who Sanctifies, Jesus. The other is the one He is sanctifying. The main goal of sanctification is to become one with Jesus.If Jesus is not ashamed to call us His brothers and sisters, on what grounds could we ever be ashamed to call Him our brother?

We should never forget that the process of sanctification is ongoing and only stops when we are called into the presence of the One Who Sanctifies, Jesus.

When we start living with Jesus, we begin to notice changes in our desires, goals, and habits; it seems the whole person is changing. The desire to learn more about God and His ways and the things He desires for our life seem to be growing every day. Even more important, we find that we, in fact, are learning and growing in God and all because of Jesus, He Who Sanctifies.

• • • • •

He Who Searches Our Hearts

And he who searches our hearts knows the mind of the Spirit, because the Spirit intercedes for the saints in accordance with God's will (Romans 8:27 NIV).

All this time, we thought that what happens in our hearts stays in our hearts. Obviously, this is not true because Jesus knows instantly what is hidden there.

When the hope in our hearts is weakened, our faith dwindles, anger wells up, we become judgmental, or our conscience starts to overtake us. Jesus—He Who Searches Our Hearts—comes to our rescue. Since He already knows the condition of our hearts, He is standing by, ready to comfort and correct the problem if we will just ask Him for His help.

Jeremiah tells us that the heart is deceitful (Jeremiah 17:9). Knowing this should make us extremely grateful to Jesus, He Who Searches Our Hearts.

We don't always understand the way to pray for our hearts' needs, but Jesus has provided us with His precious Holy Spirit to assist Him in His intercession to God on our behalf. We are being shown again the real love God has for us.

How often do we look at someone who is popular and seems to have it all together and think we would like to be in that person's place? How often do we see someone living in a palace with all the comforts of life as well as all the money they could ever need and think we would like to be in that person's place? How often do we see someone who is homeless, down and out with no visible means of even buying the next meal, and think we would never want to be in that person's place? In all these instances, we have made our decision based on outward appearances only. We know absolutely nothing about where the other person has been or is going, not to mention the relationship that other person has with God.

This, however, is where those of us who have chosen to follow Jesus are protected because Jesus is the One Who Searches Our Hearts.

The Head

Instead, speaking the truth in love, we will in all things grow up into him who is the Head, that is, Christ (Ephesians 4:15 NIV).

When it comes to the body, be it physical, spiritual, or financial, all things originate from the head.

The head is the director, if you will. It is like a command center that issues all orders. The head also is a nourishment center. If any nerve gets separated from it, that part of the body will cease to function. The head serves to unite. As close as the thumb is to the finger, neither will work together without the head.

With Jesus as our Head, He becomes our director, and His desire is to lead us into an eternity with Him. When we look at

Jesus as our command center and follow His commands, starting with the ten He gave Moses, our lives will start to take on new meaning as well as new purpose.

When we see Jesus as our source of nourishment, we start to grow and become spiritually strong in our battles, not only the battles of everyday life but those unexpected trials and challenges that seem to come out of nowhere and all but destroy us.

Only by His strength do we not get separated from the nourishment and become lost for all eternity. Remember, Jesus promised never to leave us or forsake us, and never is a long time. Jesus not only is the One who unites, but He also is the One who supplies the love that keeps families, churches, and workers at peace and allows for growth and advancement. Truly, Jesus is the Head of all things and all life.

We who love and serve Jesus must always remember that all our growth, be it physical, mental, spiritual, or financial, is because He is the Head of all aspects of our lives.

When we start to acknowledge Him in everything, depend upon Him one hundred percent for our strength and guidance, and look to Him as our only influence, we will start to think less of ourselves and more of Jesus. Then we are starting to exalt the Head, the Lord Jesus Christ.

• • • • •

The Head of All Principality and Power

And ye are complete in him, which is the head of all principality and power (Colossians 2:10 KJV).

The word *principality* implies any being in the seen as well as the unseen world. It would also include both those in support of God and His cause as well as those who oppose Him and His cause.

We should always remember that while we may call some beings demons, devils, Satan's angels, or Satan's disciples, they are all created by God. In the perfect creation, all angels are created. They, like you and me, have the right to choose whom they will serve. Satan cannot create life. He can only influence and deceive.

Jesus is still the Head of all creation; therefore, we must all give an account for our actions as well as our choices.

The word *power* implies that Jesus provides for all beings, both in the seen as well as the unseen world. This provision, depending upon our desires, can be both good and bad. If we desire to serve sin and all things evil, He will allow us to do so. Jesus has, however, made it clear that this is not the reason He died for us. His death was for our good. We must choose.

Jesus is the Head of All Principality and Power, which means no authority, ruler, or power is allowed to stand between us and Him.

Jesus is the One who comprehends, keeps, and controls all things. He is the One who keeps things in order; He is not a God of confusion.

Everyone has a choice pertaining to life, not only for our short time here on earth but also for all eternity. We can follow human wisdom as well as the false system that Satan has established, which is spiritually incomplete.

We can also follow Jesus who is complete in all phases of life both now and for all eternity. The choice is ours. The Head of All Principality and Power, Jesus, awaits our decision.

Holy One of God

And he cried out, "What have you to do with us, Jesus of Nazareth? Have you come to destroy us? I know who you are, the Holy One of God" (Mark 1:24 NRSV).

Knowing that Jesus is the Holy One of God is not enough. This unclean spirit knew who Jesus was and, in fact, knew more than the people Jesus was speaking to knew. This demon knew the power and authority that Jesus had and could use to destroy not only that demon but all the demons. In addition to knowing who Jesus is, we have to take the step that the demon refused to take. That step is to believe in Jesus, to love Him, to follow Him, to be obedient to His Word, and, with His help, to live as close a life to the one Jesus lived as possible.

Many people, then as now, follow Jesus for His miracles as well as His teachings. They accept His being the Son of God, His dying on the cross, and even His resurrection, but they stop short of total commitment to Him. They find it difficult to give all they have and are to Jesus and to deny self and follow Him.

Jesus is what every person is, a son of man. But He is also what every person should be, and that is everything God wants us to be. Jesus is the perfect pattern for us to follow. He shows compassion for the poor, the brokenhearted, the physically impaired, and the outcasts of society. Jesus wants us to be set apart as He was set apart. He doesn't want us to be corruptible and die with the world. While we will never achieve perfection on this earth, we most certainly can strive to obtain it. We must strive to live holy, pure, righteous, and godly lives, as Jesus did.

When we give our hearts and lives to Jesus without restrictions, we are in the care and protection of and under the direction of the Holy One of God.

This is significant in that Jesus is interceding on our part, and while the trip may be rough, the landing will be safe for all eternity because of Jesus, the Holy One of God.

Hope of All the World

"And his name will be the hope of all the world" (Matthew 12:21 NLT).

It would seem that this verse was written as much as a prediction as a statement of fact. More than ever, it seems the world is in great need of hope. It is hard to read a newspaper or turn on the television without being made aware that there is confusion, chaos, and unrest everywhere.

Yet those who have found a genuine relationship with Jesus have hope and confidence that all is well with them because Jesus is in control.

No matter the sin or lifestyle we may be in, if we just put our trust in Jesus, the Hope of All the World, we find peace and calmness.

Our hope becomes our belief. We no longer live in a world of maybe or could be; we live in a world of certainty—certain that Jesus will be with us regardless of life's circumstances. It doesn't matter what people say. If Jesus holds our hands, our feet will never stumble.

The world is hopeless without Jesus. If we are to have any peace or righteousness, let alone love, it will all have to come from Jesus, the Hope of All the World, because all blessings flow from this Hope.

As the Old Testament prophets hoped for things to come, they were not disappointed because God sent the Messiah. That same God promised us that this same Messiah would come back for us. Acts 1:11 (KJV) tells us, "This same Jesus who is taken up from you into heaven, shall descend in the same manner."

From His birth to His death to His resurrection, Jesus lived His life showing that He truly is the Hope of All the World.

Human Being

Instead, he gave up his divine privileges; he took the humble position of a slave and was born as a human being. When he appeared in human form (Philippians 2:7 NLT).

It is only for our benefit that Jesus made the decision to leave His place in heaven and come to earth. We must understand that Jesus did not come into existence at His human birth in Bethlehem. He has always existed as God the Son since the beginning of time. He took on human nature at His human birth but remained sinless. When we say He "took" on human form, we are saying that He added this. He did not exchange who He is. He has never ceased to be God; He simply added humanity to His divinity. He was not putting on an act when He became a servant because that is part of who He is.

At no time has Jesus ever given up His deity, not even to become human. Jesus made the decision to submit to the will of God the Father and, by doing so, limited His glory and power. He was subject to time and place; He got tired, hungry, and thirsty. He felt pain, bled, and died. His whole life on earth was one of poverty and disgrace. He was a Man of Sorrows. Had we lived in the day while He was on earth, we may well have walked by Him and never have known who He was. He was fully God and fully man at the same time. He was God manifest in human flesh.

What a blessing for us that He was. When we pray to Him about our trials, worries, fears, and concerns about tomorrow, what peace should come to us in knowing that we are not talking to someone who read a book on how to cope, but we are talking to the One who wrote the Book with the promise that He will help us. Jesus said He would be with us always if we would only trust and obey Him.

Jesus never changes, and His promises are true. Jesus was, is, and will always be God. He has always had the nature of God even when He became a human being.

NAMES OF JESUS: I

I Am

Jesus said unto them, Verily, verily, I say unto you, Before Abraham was, I am (John 8:58 KJV).

What a statement by Jesus! It is important to recognize that this is not one of the disciples or anyone else in the Bible making this statement. It is Jesus Himself. It is equally important to notice what Jesus means when He says, "Before Abraham was." Jesus does not say He was born before Abraham; He is saying that He existed before Abraham. When Jesus said that He was "I Am" to the Jewish leaders, they would have immediately tied that to what God said to Moses in Exodus 3:14. Jesus is actually saying that He is equal to God. He is stating His superiority over the prophets as well as over Abraham. In other words, divinity has no past tense and no future tense but is always the present.

There is so much in this short verse, and it caused a lot of turmoil. Jesus not only claimed to be in existence before Abraham, but He took God's holy name (I Am) and applied it to Himself. This claim by Jesus requires a response. How did the Jewish leaders respond? They wanted to stone Jesus, and they completely rejected Him. But that response did not change the truth about who Jesus is. It only established the course they selected for all eternity. As these leaders had to respond, so do we have to respond. Whatever our response is, it will establish our course for all eternity as well. God is the same yesterday, today, and forever.

What a peaceful thought that the very God who directed all

the children of Israel for forty years, protected David when he hid in the caves, and watched over Paul when his ship wrecked is the same loving, caring, and protecting God whom you and I can talk with on a regular basis.

He will provide us with the same care today as He has all the others since the beginning of time; Jesus is, in fact, I Am.

• • • • •

Intercessor

> *Who is he that condemneth? It is Christ that died, yea rather, that is risen again, who is even at the right hand of God, who also maketh intercession for us* (Romans 8:34 KJV).

What comes to mind when we think of the fact that Jesus is our Intercessor?

First, Jesus brings us to God and then puts forth the fact that He died and was resurrected for the forgiveness of our sins. He looked out from the cross and prayed for us.

Do you know someone who has faith like you have never seen, and perhaps you feel like your faith is so weak you couldn't move a feather in a windstorm? Well, guess what, Jesus prayed the same for all: both the strongest and the weakest, the healthy and the unhealthy, the orphans and the children in families, the divorced and the married, the widow and the widower as well as the married couple, those in prison as well as those who are free, the believer living on some desolate island as well as the believer living in the largest city in the world. What a glorious thought that regardless of who or what or where we are,

Jesus prayed for us and continues to intercede for us today! This very minute Jesus is still representing us. As followers of Jesus, we weren't left here by ourselves, deserted, without a leader.

No matter how high or how low we may find ourselves, remember (and you may want to write this down and keep it always available to remind you of what real help is ours) that in Romans 8:26, we are told that the indwelling Holy Spirit is praying for us. It gets better. We are told in Romans 8:31 that if God is for us, then who can be against us. His Word challenges all the trials, temptations, and demons of hell by asking who is more powerful than God.

Even better, we are told in Romans 8:34 that Jesus is making intercession for us. Note, the question of "who" in this verse is being asked to all creation from the most distant planet to the deepest part of the ocean. Every living, breathing, existing creature, be it in this physical world or the unseen world, is being asked "who?" The answer comes back loud and clear. Only One can condemn us, and that is Jesus, our Intercessor.

Is the Christ

Everyone who believes that Jesus is the Christ has become a child of God. And everyone who loves the Father loves his children too (1 John 5:1 NLT).

There are a lot of different denominations, philosophies, doctrines, and beliefs in society today. So, how do we know how to live as a true Christian, born again, child of God, overcomer of the world, sin free, or whatever term we are comfortable with? The real question is how can we be assured and have confidence in the fact that we or anyone who might ask the question will spend eternity with Jesus?

The answer is to believe that Jesus is the Christ. To believe means to put our trust, our confidence, our total being in Jesus. We are to be obedient to and believe in His Word and live with the same attitude toward and disposition and submission to God's will as Jesus did.

Don't you just love the name the Christ? Not one of many or one of a select group but the Christ. The only genuine, living, breathing, life-changing, prayer-answering, interceding, sin-forgiving, miracle-working Son of God, the Christ.

Our future is brighter because our faith is in a personal relationship with Jesus. As Jesus starts to become our friend, we will let go of the image of a historical figure or someone who might become upset and withdraw from us.

None of us have the ability to break the natural urge for power and possessions, the desire for more comforts, and the desire to put self first. No human can recreate the soul. No law can be passed, no medicine can be taken, no operation performed, no social or educational training gained that can change the soul. Nothing can change the soul but the Christ.

Things that seem impossible to us today will be routine to us tomorrow, all because of the Christ.

NAMES OF JESUS: J

Jesus

"And she will have a son, and you are to name him Jesus, for he will save his people from their sins" (Matthew 1:21 NLT).

God chose His Son's name and gave instructions that He be called by that name. No other name strikes fear into the demonic realm as does the name of Jesus.

Jesus, which means Savior, lived up to this meaning and much more. Jesus' main purpose for coming to earth was to do just what His name implies—save us.

Jesus, the Son of God, God in the flesh if you will, came near to help us, to save us, to show us how to do and follow the will of God. In no other name have people been healed, raised from the dead, and forgiven of their sins. In no other name are people being saved, being healed both physically and emotionally, and being raised from a spiritual death. In no other name are people's lives changed.

Different faiths, teachings, and religions have different person's names attached to them. Only Christianity is based totally on one person, and that is Jesus. There is no way to accept the teachings of Jesus without accepting the person, Jesus.

Jesus was His personal name. In Luke 1:31, the angel told Mary she would have a child, and His name was to be Jesus. In Matthew 1:21, an angel appeared to Joseph in a dream and told Joseph to name Mary's baby Jesus. In Matthew 1:25, we are told Mary gave birth to a baby and called Him Jesus. In Luke 2:21 at His circumcision, we are told His name was Jesus. It is well established in the biblical record that His name is Jesus, Savior, and Savior is exactly who Jesus is. We are told in Acts 16:18 that demons in the unseen world respond when given a command in the name of Jesus by those who have placed their faith in Jesus. Acts 19:13–15 tells us that demons know Jesus by name.

Some time back, a man named Pilate asked a group of people a question that had to be answered right then and there. They answered it, and they will live for all eternity with the results of their decision. The unique thing about the question is that everyone who has been born from the time Pilate asked it still has to answer that very same question today and live with the results of it.

The question is, "What shall I do then with Jesus?" (Matthew 27:22 KJV).

NAMES OF JESUS: K

The King of Israel

Nathanael answered and saith unto him, Rabbi, thou art the Son of God; thou art the King of Israel (John 1:49 KJV).

What a glorious name for Jesus!

How unnatural it seems to call a person a king who was born in a stable, worked as a carpenter, never owned any property, and had no investments that would allow Him to sit around and talk about His worldly wealth. He was ridiculed by religious and government leaders who wanted to kill Him. Yet with all these credentials, He was repeatedly called King.

We are told in Matthew 2:2 that the wise men were looking for the One who was born King. We are told in Matthew 27:37 that a sign was posted on His cross proclaiming Him as King. In John 1:49 we have a person announcing to Jesus and all those around Him that he too knows that Jesus is a King.

We normally think of a king as a leader whose major concern is to build wealth and a name for themselves and to show their power. But when we examine some of the power that Jesus, the King of Israel, displayed, we find He used His power to heal the sick. He taught that real power was to be found in loving one another. His power as King was to meet the needs of all His subjects.

Jesus, the King of Israel, having full authority and power given to Him directly by God, proclaimed as well as personally promised that if we trust in Him and obey His instructions, then whatsoever we ask of Him, we will receive; when we seek, we will find, and when we knock, it will be opened unto us (Matthew 7:7).

We are blessed by the fact that Jesus, the King of Israel, was, is, and always will be in our midst, leading and guiding us.

King of Kings

Which in his times he shall shew, who is the blessed and only Potentate, the King of kings, and Lord of lords (1 Timothy 6:15 KJV).

How do you describe someone who has no peer, who has supreme power over all creation? The Bible talks about Jesus being a King. For example, Matthew 2:2 refers to Jesus as King of the Jews. It is worthwhile to notice that Jesus did not become King of the Jews; He was born King of the Jews. Notice also that the Scripture does not just say a star but His star. Luke 19:38 refers to Jesus as the King who comes in the name of the Lord.

John 1:49 refers to Jesus as the King of Israel. This will happen when Jesus sets up His throne in Jerusalem and judges all the people and nations of the world. First Timothy 1:17 refers to Jesus as the King of the ages. Jesus will reign not only for this age but for all the ages past, present, and future. He will reign for all eternity. Revelation 15:3 refers to Jesus as the King of the nations. Do not misunderstand; this does not mean that everyone will eventually be saved. However, those who are saved will come to worship, and those who rejected Jesus will come in submission. Either way, all nations and all people will give honor and recognition to Jesus for who He is and for what He has done. Psalm 24:7 refers to Jesus as the King of glory. Jesus left the glory of heaven and came to this sin-filled world to save all humankind. He has returned to that glory, brilliance, and majestic splendor of heaven to intercede for us. Zechariah 14:9 refers to Jesus as the King of the earth.

His rule will be one of peace, tranquility, truth, and justice. His righteousness will cover the earth, and Jesus' name will be the only one worshipped. Jesus will be the only Ruler.

Jesus truly is the King of kings. While the list could go on and volumes written about His kingship, the most important title to us is Jesus, King of my heart. When we surrender total obedience, control, and direction of our lives to Jesus, we will then see Jesus quite simply as King of all kings.

• • • • •

King of Saints

And they sing the song of Moses the servant of God, and the song of the Lamb, saying, Great and marvellous are thy works, Lord God Almighty; just and true are thy ways, thou King of saints (Revelation 15:3 KJV).

Perhaps this name has more significance in heaven than it does on earth. One can't help but get a mental picture of the heavenly choir joining in with those who have gone before us, singing praise to Jesus, King of Saints.

When we think of all the Old Testament prophets, kings, judges, and those who trusted and believed in the coming Messiah, it stretches our imagination to envision the looks on their faces when they saw Jesus, the Messiah, for the first time. Just imagine the praises and conversations that must have taken place.

Yet in First Corinthians 1:2, we see Paul is calling people on earth the saints. It should not surprise anyone that God looks at anyone, living or dead, who has chosen to serve Him for all eternity as a saint. Therefore, Jesus is our King regardless of our physical condition. This most assuredly supports the fact that, living or dead, we belong to Jesus, and He will never leave us! We are His.

When we look at Romans 8:29, Galatians 4:19, and Ephesians 4:13, we start to get a clear picture of what God expects a saint to do and be. All creation owes Jesus obedience as well as gratitude for all of His provisions.

It seems, however, that we saints are to accept Him as our King. We should love Him out of spiritual fear and fear Him out of love. His love, character, and teachings should all be written in our hearts and minds.

What a glorious realization! It doesn't matter if we live or die. We are blessed with the opportunity to worship, serve, and fellowship with Jesus, King of Saints.

NAMES OF JESUS: L

Lamb of God

The next day John saw Jesus coming toward him and said, "Look! The Lamb of God who takes away the sin of the world!" (John 1:29 NLT)

What a revelation as well as a statement of fact. We find Jesus being called the Lamb of God in one other place, John 1:36. The meaning of the phrase is the main theme of the gospel in that it implies innocence, atonement for sins, redeeming power, and true obedience.

His blood is counted precious by God as well as humankind. Notice, Jesus is called the Lamb of God, not the Lamb of humankind because God gave the Lamb for sacrifice. The Lamb belongs to God.

When John 1:29 talks about "the sin," it means the sin of each one of us past, present, and future. It is as if all the sins of the world were placed in a box, and that box was placed on Jesus who took them all upon Himself and covered them with His precious blood. In turn, God accepted Jesus as a final sacrifice for our sins. He is our Savior because He is the Lamb of God.

Jesus is the total and complete Lamb of God. In the Old Testament, many lambs were sacrificed every morning and every evening in the temple for the sins of the people. The difference between those sacrifices and Jesus is wide. Jesus was perfect; the others were the best available at the time. Jesus took away our sins totally and completely. The others only represented removal and had to be repeated. Jesus took away the sins of the world, but the others were only sacrificed on behalf of the Jewish people.

Jesus has paid the price that affords us the opportunity for a sin-free and peace-loving life while here on earth as well as an opportunity to spend all eternity with Him. All we have to do is admit we are sinners in need of forgiveness. If we claim we have no sin to repent of, then we cannot receive forgiveness. Without repentance, there is no forgiveness. We need the Lamb of God.

• • • • •

Lamb on the Throne

For the Lamb on the throne will be their Shepherd. He will lead them to springs of life-giving water. And God will wipe every tear from their eyes (Revelation 7:17 NLT).

At first reading of this name, it seems a little strange that a lamb would be in such power. We generally think of a lamb as being gentle, timid, meek, and lowly in attitude and character.

However, this is the same Lamb that was led to slaughter on the cross for our sins. This is the same Lamb that we are told will be our Shepherd. We are told in Revelation 21:27 and 13:8 that He is the same Lamb who has His name on the Lamb's Book of Life.

Make no mistake thinking this Lamb will be pushed any further by sin. He will give to us according to our hearts' desires. If we desire to spend eternity with Him, His book will record our names. Our souls will face no more pain and will have complete assurance that there will be no more trials and sorrows. In fact, Revelation 21:4 tells us that God Himself will wipe away all the tears from our eyes. We are also told that all who hunger and thirst for righteousness will be filled (Matthew 5:6).

Is it possible that the Lamb's Book of Life actually has record of everything Jesus did while He was here on earth? Just think, His record is perfect, and if our names are written below His, could it be that God sees us as being perfected because of Jesus' record?

Remember, Satan knows our names but calls us by our sins. Jesus knows our sins but calls us by our names.

All of these blessings and more are because of Jesus, the Lamb on the Throne.

• • • • •

The Lamb That Was Slain
(Lamb Who Was Slaughtered)

> *Saying with a loud voice, Worthy is the Lamb that was slain to receive power, and riches, and wisdom, and strength, and honour, and glory, and blessing* (Revelation 5:12 KJV).

> *And they sang in a mighty chorus: "Worthy is the Lamb who was slaughtered—to receive power and riches and wisdom and strength and honor and glory and blessing"* (Revelation 5:12 NLT).

This is one of the most worthy names that can be ascribed to Jesus. We must remember that Jesus placed Himself in this position. He could have, at any time He chose, called armies of angels to defend Him. With His spoken word, He could have brought any type of disease, paralysis, or even death to His attackers, but He chose to die for us.

While Satan thought he had struck a permanent blow to the spiritual world and that the world, both seen and unseen, would be under his control, he, in fact, secured his own ultimate death and loss of power and control over humankind.

Notice that this verse, Revelation 5:12, tells us all the benefits that came with the Lamb being slain. These benefits become ours because of Jesus. The power of the Holy Spirit is now available to us. The riches of being able to enter into God's presence are available to us if we just ask. We are told in God's Word that any time we need wisdom, all we have to do is ask, and it will be given in abundance. We receive strength if we reach out to Jesus when we are facing some horrible trial or testing. What honor and glory are ours when we can fellowship anytime or anywhere with this blessed Trinity. God's Word tells us that, if invited, they will come and live within us. The blessings are too numerous to list.

From salvation to eternity, Jesus is with us. We don't even have to face death with fear because Jesus took dominion over death. Not only do we need never be alone again, but we need never fear that Satan can harm or rob us of anything as long as we are holding to the strong hand of Jesus. We will step from this present life right into the presence of Jesus, all of this because of the Lamb That Was Slain.

The Life

Jesus told him, "I am the way, the truth, and the life. No one can come to the Father except through me" (John 14:6 NLT).

Not only did Jesus create life, but He also made it possible to have life anew or to be born again, if you will. Jesus not only told us how we should live life; He showed us how to live life and how to live it the way God intended for humankind to live and enjoy life.

There is no other source for life here on earth or for eternity. Jesus gives life; the enemy seeks to take life. Real life begins only when we accept Jesus into our hearts. Without Jesus, we live a life of existence only. Jesus knows what life is and how it is to be lived.

When we look at Jesus through the Scriptures, we see Jesus living life the way it was intended to be lived, and we understand what is involved in living a life the way Jesus did. We see love not only in His life but in His desire to share it with others. We see joy in His life and in His spreading it to others. We see peace in Jesus' life even as He approached His death. He left that peace for all to acquire and enjoy. We see Jesus was long-suffering and instructed those who follow Him to be the same. We see gentleness in Jesus and see it everywhere He went. We see goodness in Jesus' life just by looking at all the miracles He performed. We see faith manifested to the point of death by believing in His Father's promise of resurrection. We see temperance or self-control displayed throughout Jesus' life. If we search throughout history, we find it impossible to find one to compare to Him.

In John 11:25–26, Jesus again made the claim that He is the

Life. Jesus isn't just saying that He will give life to us but that He is the Life.

What great news for the followers of Jesus, both past and present. Our loved ones who have gone on to be with Jesus aren't floating around somewhere in space, suspended in some hypnotic state or deep sleep. If they believed in Jesus, then they are with Jesus, fully alive, living in a spiritual world. The Bible calls it heaven.

The Life is now and forever. A funeral here on earth represents a welcome home party in heaven for those who love the Lord. In a heartbeat, we cease life here and start a new life there. The only condition is something that we can't work for or buy; friends or family cannot give it to us, and it is left entirely up to us. We must believe in Jesus and who He is.

Jesus asks everyone the same question that He asked Martha, "Believest thou this?" (John 11:26, KJV). If you believe Jesus, then you have the Life both now and for all eternity.

Light of Men

In him was life; and the life was the light of men (John 1:4 KJV).

Simply stated, Jesus is the creator of life, and it is His life that gives Light to men. It is a Light that enables us sinners to see ourselves as well as our need for Jesus in our lives. This Light enables us to see our way to Him so that the darkness can be removed.

When we see Jesus as the Light of Men, we are looking at

the Light of all knowledge. We see the Light of perfect love. We also see the Light of perfect doing and being.

When we use this Light to examine His life, we see a life-changing revelation because we can examine our lives beside His and start to see changes in our hearts, our desires, our thoughts, and our wills. This Light will become our conscience on decisions we make, our reason for living and being, as well as a judgment on our future and goals related to serving our Lord Jesus Christ.

Jesus is the source for all to have Light in their lives. When Jesus sheds His Light into our lives, He does so to enable us to have real life, real peace, and real love. He wants us not only to have all this but also to have it all in abundance.

We must remember that only we can turn this Light on in our lives, and we are also the only ones who can turn it off. We are the only ones who can determine how brightly we want this Light to shine. Remember, when one turns the Light off, it only stops lighting that individual's paths. No one will ever turn this Light off so that it cannot be seen. This is a Light that can never be hidden or extinguished. Jesus truly is the Light of Men.

• • • • •

Light of the World

Jesus spoke to the people once more and said, "I am the light of the world. If you follow me, you won't have to walk in darkness, because you will have the light that leads to life" (John 8:12 NLT).

Here again, we see Jesus declaring His divinity. He tells us that He is the only Light; He is the True Light. Jesus not only brings truth to light, but He also gives us the Light of spiritual understanding. He brings God Himself into the Light and shows us what God has done for us.

When we think of death, we think of darkness. Jesus has provided a way never to have to walk in darkness. By accepting Jesus as Savior and Lord of our lives, we are living in the Light. We no longer stumble around in our sins. His Light reveals our sins and our need to have our sins forgiven, and His Light directs us down the pathway of life right into eternal life with Jesus.

There are things we cannot see when we are living in spiritual darkness, like the future or life after death. We can't see God or what He is like. We stumble in darkness, looking for a purpose in this life. But when we realize our need for Light from Jesus and follow Him, we won't walk in darkness because we will have the Light.

We can't appreciate most items if they are kept in the darkness. The beauty of flowers can't be seen without light. The most beautiful picture ever painted can't be enjoyed without light. The beauty that God has instilled in us can't be seen or enjoyed by ourselves or others without the Light of Jesus. But Jesus doesn't stop with just us. He brings Light to the world, so all may see the beauty He has created and enjoy the results of His Light.

A Light to the Gentiles

A light to lighten the Gentiles, and the glory of thy people Israel (Luke 2:32 KJV).

When the Jews were looking for the Messiah, they thought He would come only for them. By declaring that Jesus is the Light to the Gentiles, Simeon, who is speaking in this verse, is saying that Jesus is the Messiah for all people who believe.

We can start each day by turning on this Light through prayer and reading His Word. The Light will expose the sin and wickedness that is in and around us, so we can then see how to clean it out of our lives.

When we realize that this Light is near us now and will remain near us for all eternity, we start to see clearly the path Jesus wants us to take. Not only do we see the path, but also we are able to see the character of God, His plan of redemption, His love and concern for us, and His plan to prosper us and not to harm us. Fear is no longer part of daily life.

We are no longer ignorant of Satan's plans and schemes. Satan's lies are exposed for what they are, and temptation becomes something we can see and control with the help of Jesus.

As the Light gets brighter in our lives, we start to mature in new areas. We learn the real meaning and implementation of love. Our knowledge is increased, and we start to notice the real meaning of life.

What a beautiful thought! We can live in the Light now and for all eternity. In the Light, not only are we able to see and understand what we are doing and where we are going, but Jesus can see us as well.

The Lily of the Valleys

I am the rose of Sharon, and the lily of the valleys (Song of Songs 2:1 KJV).

What a lovely description of our Lord and Savior, Jesus!

When we see a lily, we see a beautiful white flower that represents purity. Who is more pure than Jesus? He never entertained an evil thought or said or did anything wrong.

The design of the lily is such that the head is drooping and sits behind the leaves that surround it. It doesn't push itself forward. Emblematically, it reminds us of the lowliness and humility of Jesus.

When we are near a lily, we are pleased and delighted by its color as well as the sweet fragrance that surrounds us. We should find ourselves experiencing the same when we are in the presence of Jesus.

Notice that Jesus is the Lily of the Valleys, not the valley. Generally speaking, the word *valley* is accepted as meaning a low spot in our lives. When we are experiencing these valleys, there stands our Lily, and we know by His sweet fragrance that He is with us, bringing joy and pleasure as well as delight to us.

Jesus is a delight to see when we look for Him in faith. He brings with Him peace and rest for our travels through the valleys. Jesus is a joy to see and hear when it seems no one else understands us, let alone has ever gone through what we are going through.

As our physical senses are trained to recognize sights, sounds, and smells, so must our spiritual senses be trained to recognize that which is pleasing in the spiritual realm. What a glorious thought that when we start into a valley, we have there beside us the Lily of that valley.

Living One

I am the living one. I died, but look—I am alive forever and ever! And I hold the keys of death and the grave (Revelation 1:18 NLT).

What a fantastic statement, especially for the followers of Jesus, in view of the fact that Jeremiah 23:36 tells us God the Father is alive. What a grand declaration that Jesus has spoken! We don't serve a dead idol or some non-thinking, non-speaking, non-acting, non-hearing, non-seeing, non-caring object. We serve a living God who is always with us, is in control of our lives, and is concerned about every aspect of our lives. Jesus has set up a system whereby we can have our sins forgiven, our lives changed, our bodies healed, and an eternal life with Him.

Why is it important to us that Jesus is the Living One? Because He created everything and has control over everything. He knows us by name. We are told in His Word that the Living One we serve searches the whole earth just so He can strengthen those of us whose lives are totally committed to Him. If that doesn't excite you, then call an ambulance because you are almost dead, or, in this case, grab your Bible and start reading; you need fuel in your spiritual tank.

There is only one living God. Over the years, humankind has served other gods made from various materials and objects, and some have worshiped other persons. However, none of these gods can forgive humankind of sin or save us from death and judgment.

When we place our hope for forgiveness and a life of eternity with the Living One, it is not hope placed on a possibility, on a philosophy, on some material object, or on a set of rules.

It is hope placed on Jesus, the One who came to earth, who

taught us how to live for God, died for our sins, and arose victorious over sin and death to give us the certainty of eternal life. Jesus is the Creator of humankind and the sustainer of humankind as well as humankind's provider. He is working and acting within us right now, and if we continue to be committed to Jesus and are totally obedient to Him, we will see the Living One, face to face, and live with Jesus forever.

Lord

If anyone asks what you are doing, just say, "The Lord needs them," and he will immediately let you take them (Matthew 21:3 NLT).

As Lord, Jesus showed His omniscience by telling the disciples exactly where to find the donkey and its colt and that the owners would have no problem in the disciples taking them.

As our Lord, He is the only One who can stand between us and God. He is the One who created all things with God the Father. It is by Him that we are saved. He is our Redeemer. He is the Savior of the world. He is in us, and we are in Him. Every good and perfect gift comes from Him. He is our source of life.

When we look at the name *Jesus*, we see the Man. When we look at the name *Christ*, we see the Redeemer. When we look at the name *Lord*, we see the strength that brings us before God Himself.

God has seen to it that every king, authority, person, race, belief, creed, religion, man, woman, child, nation, and language will confess that Jesus is Lord. Every creature will worship Him for who He is and who He claimed to be when He walked upon this earth—the Son of the Living God, the Lord of the universe. Every knee shall bow, and every tongue shall confess that fact.

If Jesus is Lord of our lives, then each crisis should become an opportunity to witness about His greatness. We should turn our lives over to Him and live to please, honor, and glorify Him. We should live with a desire to do His will and to be obedient to Him regardless of our circumstances and in spite of the consequences. Give Jesus all the honor and glory due Him, and as your Lord, He will give you His power, His wisdom, His goodness, His faithfulness, and His promises.

All will serve as a defense and will assist against any attacks that might be brought on you. Jesus truly is our friend if we follow His direction. He is our Lord only if we are obedient to Him.

Lord Jesus Christ

This letter is from James, a slave of God and of the Lord Jesus Christ. I am writing to the "twelve tribes"—Jewish believers scattered abroad. Greetings! (James 1:1 NLT)

Of all the millions of names that have been given since God first named man and woman, none comes close to comparing to this one name. Just saying the name makes you feel better. You feel more secure, more confident, more assured that everything is going to be okay, and that comes from just speaking the name, Lord Jesus Christ. Think of what positive results are ahead when we invoke this name against the trials and tribulations of everyday life. When these names are used together, they show the confidence we have in the person we are trusting with our lives, not just for a few short years here on earth but for all eternity.

As Lord, He is the One who will return to this earth in all His glory. As Jesus, He is the One who came to earth as a human being to show us how to live as God the Father wants us to. As Christ, He is the One who died on the cross to fulfill God's plan and purpose for us.

There was a time when calling someone Lord was considered treason by the government and blasphemous by religious leaders.

Over the course of human history, thousands have lost their lives because they would not retract the claim that Jesus is Lord. Today, it seems that using Jesus' name is more for bumper stickers or slogans. People seem more concerned about being politically correct than they are in being biblically correct.

It is hard to imagine thousands willing to die just to be able to speak the name Lord Jesus Christ, while so many are silent as His name is being silenced in public. His image is not allowed on public grounds. An elected official can openly claim a lifestyle of homosexuality and moral decay and can pursue a not-so-subtle drive to eliminate any type of reference about God. Many vote to remove a lifestyle that would oppose them, and silence is all that is heard from those who claim to be followers of the Lord Jesus Christ.

It was easy for James to declare that he was a servant to Jesus because of all he had seen and experienced in his life with Him. We should be able to take the same position as James and for the same reasons. We know the Lord Jesus Christ.

Lord of All

This is the message of Good News for the people of Israel—that there is peace with God through Jesus Christ, who is Lord of all (Acts 10:36 NLT).

This is perhaps one of the most comforting verses in the Bible. It shows that Jesus doesn't care who you are, where you are from, or what your political or financial standing is. He wants to be part of your life.

In Romans 14:9, we are told that Jesus is Lord of the living and the dead. This is one of the many reasons Jesus died and arose. It doesn't matter if we are living or have gone on to heaven; Jèsus is our Lord. If we are really committed to Jesus, have asked Him into our life, have accepted Him, and are serving Him in obedience, then we belong to Him. We no longer have the right to make decisions about our attitudes and actions that would oppose those of Jesus. The reason for our desire to serve Him and be obedient to Him is that He purchased the right to our life and death by His death.

In 1 Timothy 6:15, we are told Jesus is the Lord of all lords. It is only by His will and approval that we exist and will be allowed into His kingdom. In 1 Corinthians 2:8, we are told that Jesus is the Lord of Glory. Jesus came to earth to save us from sin, not just while on earth but for all eternity.

Jesus is Lord of all powers, principalities, and might, not only in this world as we know it but also in any world as yet unseen. Jesus is and will continue to be for all eternity Lord of All, including heaven. Jesus has never had nor will ever have an equal or anyone who even comes close to being compared to Him, except of course God the Father and God the Holy Spirit. Knowing that Jesus is Lord of All should give us peace that cannot be purchased. Wherever Jesus goes, we who serve Him will go with Him, and wherever we go, Jesus will go with us.

Love

God's love was revealed among us in this way: God sent his only Son into the world so that we might live through him (1 John 4:9 NRSV).

No other word is tied so closely to love than the word *Jesus*. The greatest proof of God's love for us is His Son, Jesus. How can we not love one another when Jesus went to such lengths to love humankind even though we opposed Him, ignored Him, cursed Him, rejected Him, persecuted Him, and killed Him? Even after all that, Jesus still loves us and stands ready to forgive us of our sins.

Love explains why God created humankind. God wanted to love us, and since God loves us, He wants to care for us as well. God wants a loving response from humankind. That is why we are free to choose if we want to love and serve Him. The love that Jesus has for humankind is what put Him on the cross. It was the solution to the problem of sin in humankind's life. When love is spoken, it is unproven. When love is put into action, it is not only seen but also is fully proven and understood. It cannot be called anything other than what it is seen to be.

When we talk about loving God, it is just talk. But when we start to pray for one another, lend a helping hand to others, help feed and clothe the needy, stop seeking revenge, stop trying to make sure that we are number one in our lives, and put others' needs ahead of our needs, then God will see love in our lives.

When we let God have complete control of our lives and, with Jesus' help, try to be obedient to His Word, love can't help but show itself. Everywhere we go and in everything we say and do, love will be seen and heard.

God, whom no person has ever seen, somehow becomes visible in the lives of those who really start to love one another. First John 4:12 tells us that God's love is perfected in us if we love one another. Since we did absolutely nothing to deserve God's love, why should our fellow humans have to do something to deserve ours? When we claim to be Christians, we are claiming to have the love of God living in us.

NAMES OF JESUS: M

A Man Approved of God

Ye men of Israel, hear these words; Jesus of Nazareth, a man approved of God among you by miracles and wonders and signs, which God did by him in the midst of you, as ye yourselves also know (Acts 2:22 KJV).

There are many ways that God showed His approval of His Son, Jesus. There is the public approval of Jesus by God at Jesus' baptism (Matthew 3:17), at His Transfiguration (Luke 9:35), and while Jesus was teaching (John 12:29). Jesus performed many miracles and works that proved God was working through Him. We are told in Acts 13:30 that "God raised him from the dead" (KJV).

We are fully aware that Jesus now sits at the right hand of God interceding on our behalf. If God did not approve of everything Jesus said, did, and thought as well as the way He acted and lived His life while here on earth, Jesus would not be in the very presence of God the Father now. Perhaps one of God's greatest means of showing His approval was sending the precious Holy Spirit to comfort and lead us just as Jesus had promised.

The miracles in our lives certainly attest to God's approval of His Son, our salvation being one of these miracles.

Being able to live with peace in our lives and an assurance that all is well for eternity, not only for us but also for our loved ones, is a daily reminder that Jesus is a Man Approved of God.

Man of Sorrows

He was despised and rejected—a man of sorrows, acquainted with deepest grief. We turned our backs on him and looked the other way. He was despised, and we did not care (Isaiah 53:3 NLT).

One way Jesus was to be recognized when He came to earth is that He was to be a Man of Sorrows. His life of sorrow would be the power that drew others to Him. It would not be His charm or cheerfulness, pleasant speech, or happy character but His closeness to sorrow. When we look at Jesus' personal life, we see sorrow. Jesus had left heaven and was away from His Father. He was unable as a young man to share what was really inside Him or to open up His mind and share His thoughts. If He had, who would have understood them? This had to make Jesus a lonely man.

Jesus found joy within Himself, knowing what the end result of all His sorrow would be. Hebrews 12:2 tells us He looked at the cross with joy. What could possibly cause someone getting ready to face such a horrible death to look at it with joy? For Jesus, it was easy because through His eyes He saw no more sin, no more crippled, blind, or muted people, or sickness of any kind. Broken homes, even death, would be under His control; peace would be restored to the world, and love would be found in all nature as well as humankind. Most importantly of all, every human being would now have access to God; they would be able to walk, talk, and come into His very presence for all eternity.

Yes, Jesus is a Man of Sorrows and is acquainted with grief. It is through this that we are called His children and can be sure He knows each one of us by name.

Jesus replied, "If anyone loves me, he will obey my teaching. My Father will love him, and we will come to him and make our home with him" John 14:23 (NIV).

• • • • •

Man Who Healed

But he replied, "The man who healed me told me, 'Pick up your mat and walk'" (John 5:11 NLT).

What a sad situation we have here. A man has just had a life-changing event take place in his life, but one of the first things he does when questioned about the miracle is to blame Jesus instead of praising Him. The next thing we notice is that he doesn't even know the name of the miracle worker. Obviously, in his heart, he had no intention of thanking Him for the miracle.

When God touches our bodies, be it physical or mental healing, or meets a need of any kind, we need to be careful not to get so caught up in what has happened that we fail to spend more time thanking Him for the miracle than we did asking Him for it.

We also notice that they were ignorant about true authority. It should have been obvious to them that God had healed this man. In turn, they should have been excited about finding and talking with Jesus. Their thoughts were centered on their own position and authority. All they cared about was maintaining a routine, and they were going to do whatever they could to maintain it. Dead religion is not a religion of love and concern. The Pharisees ask this question, "Who is the man that broke our law concerning the Sabbath?" The real question should have been, "Who is the man who loved you and was concerned about you?" When Jesus is taken out of religion and our lives, all that is left is a feeling of insecurity. We feel threatened that someone else may have more power or influence over things than we do.

While we can blame churches, pastors, Sunday school teachers, Christians, even God Himself, the bottom line is that it doesn't matter who or what we blame. We are responsible for our own souls.

We are the only ones responsible for where we will spend eternity. What type of relationship we will have with Jesus, the Man Who Heals, is our decision alone.

• • • • •

Master

And they came to him, and awoke him, saying, Master, master, we perish. Then he arose, and rebuked the wind and the raging of the water: and they ceased, and there was a calm (Luke 8:24 KJV).

When most of us hear the word *master*, there is an instant rejection. The idea of having to be obedient as well as having to explain our actions and our decisions generally does not sit well with us. It is, however, impossible for humankind to be without some type of master.

The word master implies, in most cases, someone or something in authority or someone or something that teaches. When the name Master is applied to Jesus, it means teacher. Human masters, for example, use words to teach. Jesus imparts His spirit. Human masters can establish and direct schools. Only Jesus can found and direct the church. While God is the believers' only Father, Jesus is their only Master.

Our master will be what our hearts love and desire. Those who love God hate the world. Those who love the world hate God. When we try and mingle the two, we find that both are not enjoyable. One of the reasons for this is that God requires total commitment and service to Him. He requires a total commitment of the heart as well.

When we, with open minds, examine and study God and His Word, we find God to be the One who gives the real life as well as a meaning to it. It takes but a short time to learn that He supplies all of our needs. He does not necessarily supply all of our wants and desires, but that is because of His unconditional love for us. The question we have to ask ourselves is does the master we now serve last throughout all eternity? Is this master real?

Is this master one that we trust with our businesses, families, and friends, as well as our lives? If we are serving the Master whom God sent, then the answer is a resounding yes because that Master is His Son, Jesus.

• • • • •

Master of the Household

Students are to be like their teacher, and slaves are to be like their master. And since I, the master of the household, have been called the prince of demons, the members of my household will be called by even worse names! (Matthew 10:25 NLT).

What great news for those of us who love Jesus—Jesus has called us to be part of His family. With that thought in mind, what can the world say to us or call us that would do anything other than draw us closer to Jesus? Regardless of what is said about us, it will not change the calling God has placed on our lives. It will make it an even higher calling. Just think, we are being placed in the same category as Jesus. That does not mean, however, that we should speak before we think. Looking for ridicule is not a way of serving God. What we are being told by Jesus is that the servant is not greater than the master.

Jesus is simply telling us to pay attention and not think we are the only ones who will go through difficult times just so we can be obedient to God the Father. His point is that the demons know who Jesus is and by what authority He was sent. Thanks be to God! The same protection, love, knowledge, and care that surrounded and lived in Jesus is available to us.

That same patience, calmness, and assurance that Jesus showed is ours as well. The same source that Jesus relied upon is ours to rely upon and call upon. The same Holy Spirit that led and directed and was available to Jesus is available to us.

No one has ever asked Jesus to be a teacher, counselor, and provider without asking Him to come into his or her heart and life as Lord and Savior.

Jesus wants to become Master of our Household. "Let this mind be in you, which was also in Christ Jesus" (Philippians 2:5, KJV).

• • • • •

Messenger

So Jesus told them, "My message is not my own; it comes from God who sent me" (John 7:16 NLT).

What a phenomenal claim Jesus made! He was sent by God to be His Messenger. The message was from God, and God was the source of all Jesus' knowledge. Because of the intimate relationship He had and continues to have with God, Jesus was and is qualified to deliver the message.

The way to test Jesus' message is the same way we should test every message we hear regardless of who the speaker is. It is a simple yet fail-proof test. The words of the message should not contradict what the Bible tells us. They should be in complete agreement. The speaker's words should point directly to God and His will for our lives, never the will of the speaker. A messenger should not throw around titles or credentials or be preoccupied with set programs and procedures. While structure and order must be maintained in worshiping God, they should never prohibit the moving of the Holy Spirit. Whatever level of success is achieved, all credit should go to God, not to the messenger. Jesus brought a message that would not only change the lives of those around Him at that time but would forever change the lives of everyone until He returns.

The message took all the responsibility out of the law, rituals, ceremonies, and sacrifices. It put the responsibility for our relationship with God squarely on each and every individual from the time Jesus came to earth until He returns. There never was, is, or will be a valid reason for not giving our lives to Jesus and serving and being obedient to Him. Regardless of your position in society, your educational level, financial standing, or nationality, only one reason keeps people from accepting God's message, and that is, "I don't want anything to do with this One called the Son of God, the Lord Jesus Christ."

The message brought by the Messenger whom God sent is still the same message. What will your answer be?

Messenger of the Covenant

"Look! I am sending my messenger, and he will prepare the way before me. Then the Lord you are seeking will suddenly come to his Temple. The messenger of the covenant, whom you look for so eagerly, is surely coming," says the Lord of Heaven's Armies (Malachi 3:1 NLT).

As the Messenger of the Covenant, Jesus would reform the world spiritually as no one else ever had or ever will. He came to reform humankind's habits, emotions, beliefs, thoughts, lifestyles, and goals.

Jesus' coming fulfilled the covenant made with Abraham that all the people on earth should be blessed in his seed.

As the Messenger of the Covenant, Jesus fulfilled both the Old and the New Testament claims and prophecies. Notice in Malachi 3:2, we get a glimpse of this Messenger. The question is asked, who can on their own stand before Him? In this verse, reference to the refiner's fire and fullers' soap implies the need to destroy corrupt ingredients that are mixed in with non-corrupt and the need to clean all filthy garments of the dirt attached to them. Jesus, through His reformation, cleans and destroys everything that is impure, wrong, and unclean—anything in our souls that would be in opposition to God's will and ways. Jesus will not stop, as long as we continue to invite Him into our lives, until He has us cleaned to the point that when He looks at us He sees His reflection in us. This covenant is a verbal covenant on our part, and we are free to break it anytime we want. However, Jesus neither can nor will break this covenant.

Jesus signed this covenant with His blood, and it cost Him His life. Failure on our part to sign this covenant will cost us our eternal life.

• • • • •

Mighty Warrior

> *But the Lord is with me like a mighty warrior; so my persecutors will stumble and not prevail. They will fail and be thoroughly disgraced; their dishonor will never be forgotten* (Jeremiah 20:11 NIV).

When we think of a warrior, we generally think of a strong, powerful person, skilled and very dangerous or very comforting, depending on what side of the battle you are on.

As followers of Jesus, a Mighty Warrior, we have a real advantage over our enemy. We have been given the battle plan as well as the tools to fight with. Perhaps the greatest advantage we possess is that we know not only how but also who wins the final battle.

No matter how powerful or evil the enemy might seem, our Mighty Warrior, Jesus, is more powerful. We must never forget that the one we are fighting was created by Jesus. We must never forget that when we give our lives to Jesus, God considers us His own. With that knowledge, we must be confident that when Satan attacks us and comes against us, he is attacking and coming against God Himself. How comforting not just to think it but know for a fact that God the Father, God the Son, and God the Holy Spirit go before us. Not only when we are in a major battle but every second of our lives, the Trinity surrounds us and watches over us. Oh, let us not forget the thousands and thousands of angels the Trinity has to call upon to look after us as well. It almost makes one want to go out and start a fight with Satan just to see him run in fear.

There is nothing or no one, no manmade god in the earthly or spiritual world, who could, can, or will ever defeat God or stop Him from executing His final plan for our lives. God will fulfill all of His promises, and He will fulfill them because of Jesus, a Mighty Warrior.

My Helper

> *So that we may boldly say, The Lord is my helper, and I will not fear what man shall do unto me* (Hebrews 13:6 KJV).

How very, very personal this name is. Jesus is not just a helper for a certain race or certain thing or a certain length of time, but He is My Helper for all things and for all time.

When we really understand that Jesus is My Helper, we then become content in life. Instead of constantly struggling to obtain more, we become content with what we have because we realize that Jesus supplies all of our needs.

We no longer need to live in fear because My Helper is present. He is permanent in our lives and assists against all troubles. Remember, people can only come against us to the point God allows. We need not let our thoughts take possession of our faith. Jesus is not only My Helper, but He is also our protector as well as our provider and Friend.

We must remember that Jesus is our Helper. The very name helper implies that we have to be busy doing something, or we wouldn't need help.

If we could learn to be on a first-name basis with My Helper, if we could develop such a habit that talking with Him is not reserved for times of crisis only, if we would talk to Him when we don't need something, or if we would just thank Him for all His love routinely, then we would become filled with confidence and boldness. We would know that when we no longer can complete the tasks, My Helper can and will.

My Helper, Jesus, is infinite in His wisdom. His grace is inexhaustible. He is always with us. We can come to Him anytime. His desire and willingness to help us is as great as His love. Remember, His love for us caused His death on the cross.

His promises are as real and true today as they were the day He spoke them. Not only is He our strength, protection, and provider, but He is our Healer. Jesus is My Helper in all phases of our lives.

• • • • •

My Lord and My God

And Thomas answered and said unto him, My Lord and my God (John 20:28 KJV).

Wow! What a personal statement not only for Thomas to make but for us to make as well. In effect, we are saying, "My Lord," the One to whom I totally and completely surrender my life, as well as "My God," the One whom I believe without reservation.

When we read Thomas's story in the Bible, we come away calling him "doubting Thomas." Interestingly enough, however, Jesus didn't challenge Thomas for his doubting. Jesus challenged him for his unbelief.

How often are we guilty of refusing to believe, in faith, what God's Word says and demanding that He prove it before we will believe it? How often do we say that if certain things happen, then we will go to church or start tithing or become believers?

But just as Jesus came down to Thomas's level, He will come down to ours if we seek Him with sincere hearts.

Thomas took a scientific approach to his spiritual life, and it didn't work. When people make a statement that they won't believe unless this or that happens, at that very point, they are admitting that they do believe. They have placed their belief in the results of a test that they devised. If they can have faith in this test, then they can have faith in Jesus' teachings.

Remember, when we wish that we could physically touch Jesus or sit down for a face-to-face physical conversation and get His counsel, we should stop and thank God that He, in His infinite wisdom, devised a far greater plan that doesn't limit Him to one physical body. He wants to be with everyone all the time.

Like us, when Thomas really saw Jesus, he was no longer "doubting" Thomas, but, like us, he became "believing" Thomas. Thomas's response, like ours when we see Jesus as He truly is, acknowledges that He truly is our Lord and our God.

NAMES OF JESUS: N

Name Above All Other Names

> *Therefore, God elevated him to the place of highest honor and gave him the name above all other names* (Philippians 2:9 NLT).

This verse may seem a little confusing at first, but once you look at what this verse is really saying, you get blessed many times over. This name talks more about the person Jesus than it does a title. Jesus' dignity and honor as well as His versatility and ability to be all things to all people are being expressed here. To get to the position that He now holds, Jesus did not insist on His equality with God; instead, He willingly and desirably was obedient to God's plan for humankind's salvation. In return, God rewarded Jesus' obedience by bestowing upon Him the Name Above All Other Names.

To Christians, Jesus' name is loved because by His name our sins are forgiven. We are assured that we can enter into the very presence of God by His name.

In Genesis, Abraham called on the name of the Lord. In Exodus, the Lord proclaimed His own name to Moses. In Leviticus, Israel was warned not to profane the name of the Lord. In Deuteronomy, the priests were to minister in the name of the Lord. In Judges, the name of God was called Wonderful. In Genesis, we are told that to call on the name of the Lord is to worship Him as God. We are told in John that salvation comes through His name. In Matthew, we are told that believers are to gather in His name. In John, we are told that our prayers are to be made in His name. In Matthew, we are told that those who follow and serve Him and bear His name will be hated. In Acts, we are told to worship in His name, serve in His name, and suffer in His name. In Philippians, we are told that in His name, some day, every knee will bow and every tongue will confess that Jesus Christ is Lord. As we can see, if we look in either the Old Testament or the New Testament, we see the holy character of the One we serve.

There never has been nor ever will be a name that can be compared with His name. It stands alone. Jesus is our Savior. Jesus only is Christ. Jesus is the only Son of God. All of Jesus' titles, positions, character, dignity, and goals are above all others, truly a Name Above All Other Names.

• • • • •

New Covenant

> *But when God found fault with the people, he said: "The day is coming, says the LORD, when I will make a new covenant with the people of Israel and Judah"* (Hebrews 8:8 NLT).

When we come to God, we are coming through the New Covenant, the Lord Jesus Christ. When we accept Jesus, we are accepting the terms of the New Covenant. We believe that Jesus is the living Son of God who came to earth and died on the cross for our sins, was buried and arose three days later victorious over death and sin, and now sits at the right hand of God the Father.

Some awesome things happen when we accept this New Covenant. God will renew our minds by putting His laws in our minds. He will also renew our hearts and write His laws on our hearts.

With our new hearts and minds, we now have a strong desire to follow and obey God and the power to do so. We have this power and desire even when we fail Him and fall short, and let me assure you that we will fail more than we would like to admit. But with renewed hearts and minds, we will ask for and receive His forgiveness then continue seeking after Him and being obedient to His Word. Remember, when God forgives our sins, it is because of His mercy rather than any law or anything we do.

Forgiveness simply means that God no longer remembers our sins. We often remember them, and without a doubt, Satan remembers them because he is constantly throwing them up to us and causing us to question if they really have been forgiven. Why do you think he is called the accuser? God, however, puts them out of His mind. We are told He never thinks back on them. Through the New Covenant, our sins are completely and totally forgiven and forgotten.

We must never forget that God rejected Israel because they were disobedient to the old covenant. It should be clear then that God will reject us as well if we are disobedient to the New Covenant, His Son, Jesus.

NAMES OF JESUS: O

Offering for Our Sins

For God made Christ, who never sinned, to be the offering for our sin, so that we could be made right with God through Christ (2 Corinthians 5:21 NLT).

Can you imagine being born for no other reason than to die for someone you never personally met or knew? Add to that having everyone who ever lived place all their sins on you. In addition, all the punishment that should have been given to them is placed on you.

Now, in order to accomplish this, you must not sin, not even in thought; you must love everyone, even those who will lie about you, nail you to a cross, laugh at you, and mock you as you die. Then you must, out of genuine love and desire, return to your home and plead for all those who still reject you. That pleading is for forgiveness, protection, healing, and provision for all their needs. While this scenario may sound ludicrous, that is exactly what Jesus did and is still doing for us.

Without the heart and love of Jesus in our lives, it is impossible to comprehend what God, through Jesus, did for us.

This verse, which proclaims the depth of love that God has for us, is one of the greatest verses in the entire Bible. We could perhaps spend a lifetime studying just this one verse and still not comprehend the real love of God.

God loves His Son, Jesus, to such depths that anyone who loves His Son by believing in Him and the price He paid will be forgiven of their sins and will spend all eternity with Jesus. God exchanges that belief for the price Jesus paid on the cross, and we become justified and able to come into God's presence and communicate with Him—because of this one Offering for Our Sins.

* * * * *

One Who Existed from the Beginning

We proclaim to you the one who existed from the beginning, whom we have heard and seen. We saw him with our own eyes and touched him with our own hands. He is the Word of life (1 John 1:1 NLT).

Why is it important to us that Jesus has always existed and was not created but has always been with God the Father and God the Holy Spirit? Would it really matter if God would have created Jesus just for the purpose of the cross? The answer is yes, a thousand times over, yes. Jesus' presence at the creation of the heavens and earth and the creation of all life, including humankind, allows us to know with confidence that Jesus spoke with truth and firsthand knowledge about God and heaven. Therefore, we can trust His Word and Him as well. If Jesus were created solely for the cross, what choice would He have had? Where would the love and compassion that Jesus showed while here on earth and continues to show today come from? Remember, we serve a living, breathing, thinking, speaking, seeing, and acting God, not some mechanical, non-feeling god.

Why is it so easy to believe other eyewitnesses to history, yet when it comes to the life of Jesus, doubt, disbelief, and even wars rage over this historical event? One reason there is so much doubt, disbelief, and confusion is that no other event comes close to having such an impact on our lives as this one small span of time in history.

John's account is given to us by an eyewitness to everything that happened to Jesus. The choice becomes ours as to whether or not we choose to accept Jesus as the true living Son of God who was with God before creation and still lives today.

Yes, Jesus has always existed. He is living and will intercede on our behalf until He returns to claim His own.

He is the power and source of life itself. That is why we can have and enjoy life to the fullest now and for all eternity—because Jesus is the One Who Existed from the Beginning.

● ● ● ● ●

The One Who Is Speaking

Be careful that you do not refuse to listen to the One who is speaking. For if the people of Israel did not escape when they refused to listen to Moses, the earthly messenger, we will certainly not escape if we reject the One who speaks to us from heaven! (Hebrews 12:25 NLT)

There are two distinctions between two people here. One is Moses; the other, Jesus. The first distinction is where they spoke from. Moses spoke on earth what was given to him by God in heaven. Moses was a mouthpiece, if you will. Through Moses, God gave humankind His law. Jesus, however, spoke and continues to speak from heaven. He is the voice of God Himself. The second distinction is in the possibility for error. With Moses, humankind may argue that perhaps he misunderstood or got some of it wrong, but with Jesus, there is no room for misunderstanding or for a chance that He got it wrong. We have the availability of Jesus and the opportunity to speak with Him anytime and about anything.

People may say that there is no God in an effort to live in sin and try to avoid conviction. But true atheists are either spiritually foolish (Psalm 14:1) or so full of evil that they have hardened their hearts to the point that God has rejected them. A person may be of high educational intelligence but foolish in the education of the soul. We need to be cautious that we don't depend more on ourselves than we do Jesus. In effect, we become atheists in a fashion. Jesus wants us to place all of our cares on Him. We need to trust and obey Him in every phase of our lives.

Most of us have, at one time or another, been told to pay attention, and we might learn something. Never is this statement more applicable than when it applies to Hebrews 12:25. We need to listen, receive, and obey the One Who Is Speaking, which is Jesus.

The One Who Was Dead but Is Now Alive

> *"Write this letter to the angel of the church in Smyrna. This is the message from the one who is the First and the Last, who was dead but is now alive"* (Revelation 2:8 NLT).

What is so significant about this name is that Jesus Himself is claiming it. This name implies many things. Perhaps one of the biggest is that Jesus fulfilled His promise. In doing so, Jesus assures us that everything He ever said was and is true.

We need never worry about our salvation or where we will spend eternity because Jesus has promised us that He is in complete control. The fear of death has been erased and replaced with a new confidence. Jesus has personally experienced both pain and death; not only did He gain victory over them, but He also now has complete control over them. Jesus showed us that death is nothing more than a phase in life through which we must go.

What a comfort to know that He is not a dead hero whom we need to make attempts to remember. Jesus is alive and is with us every moment of our lives now and for all eternity. He is in complete control if we allow Him to be. He is the same Jesus who died and was resurrected; He arose from the dead as an example for us. That example now becomes a promise that those who have committed their lives to Him will do the same.

Many things in life bring a tremendous amount of joy: falling in love, marrying and spending a lifetime with your best friend; being involved in creating a new life; watching that life grow and develop into something that you can be proud of now; and knowing you will spend all eternity with your loved ones.

There is no greater joy than that of knowing that we serve and are loved by the One Who Was Dead but Is Now Alive.

● ● ● ● ●

The One with the Sharp Two-edged Sword

"Write this letter to the angel of the church in Pergamum. This is the message from the one with the sharp two-edged sword" (Revelation 2:12 NLT).

Notice that Jesus is describing Himself as the One with the Sharp Two-edged Sword. He does not say a sword or a sharp sword. He is precise in saying that He has a sharp two-edged sword. As with everything Jesus said in His teachings, even in His parables, He was precise and specific to His point. We would be wise not to ignore His Word.

God's Word is sharp; it has the ability to cut the most hardened sin away from even the most hardened sinner, leaving a clean, fresh heart to beat for the cause of Jesus.

When we look at this two-edged sword, we see on one side the law of God and the need to live a godly life in order to avoid His judgment. On the other side of the sword, we see God's love and peace to those who choose to follow Jesus and not the world.

Jesus is telling us that His Word is more powerful than any weapon the world can create. For those who follow Jesus, what a glorious thought; how wonderful that news is! Jesus is more powerful than any trial, temptation, or attack of the enemy. No matter what, Jesus will protect and defend us and meet our every need. Perhaps the greatest power that His Word provides is that, on His Word, we leave this world and enter into the presence of God for all eternity.

We don't have to worry about Satan trying to get us to believe his lies. Satan's lies may be that we cannot be sure that our sins have been forgiven or that we have been so evil that God could not forgive us.

It doesn't matter what the accuser, Satan, tries to get you to believe or what some well-meaning follower of Jesus may say. There are two people who really know the truth. It is on this knowledge of truth that your eternity is based. You are one of the two who knows what is really in your heart and how you really feel toward God. The other One who knows what is in your heart is the One with a Sharp Two-edged Sword, Jesus.

• • • • •

One Witness

"Your own law says that if two people agree about something, their witness is accepted as fact. I am one witness, and my Father who sent me is the other" (John 8:17–18 NLT).

Here is one name that actually needs very little written about it. We all know what a witness is—someone who sees something happen, records that event, and then repeats it so that can bring either good or bad results. We should never lose sight of the fact that Jesus knows all about our lives as well as our actions.

It seems strange in some ways that we will ask God to hear our prayers. We cry out in such need that it seems we can hardly bear it, and we want Jesus to be closer than a brother to us. At other times, though, we wish that we could just act or speak in a way that God can't hear. Either way, we must always know that Jesus is One Witness.

The Rabbinic laws talk about the need for two witnesses. However, in Jesus' case, only God the Father could witness about Him.

We notice that when Jesus was baptized, God and the Holy Spirit were witnesses (Matthew 3:16–17). We see two witnesses at His Transfiguration, Moses and Elijah (Luke 9:28–31). John 20:11–12 tells us that two angels witnessed His resurrection.

Perhaps the greatest witnesses were the two angels who guaranteed Jesus' return (Acts 1:9–11).

When we start to get weak in our faith or wonder if the life we chose following Jesus is the right one, we have two of the greatest witnesses we can ever hope or pray to have (John 8:18).

We who serve and live for Jesus are vindicated by One Witness, Jesus.

Our Passover Lamb

Get rid of the old "yeast" by removing this wicked person from among you. Then you will be like a fresh batch of dough made without yeast, which is what you really are. Christ, our Passover Lamb, has been sacrificed for us (1 Corinthians 5:7 NLT).

Without this act of sacrifice by Jesus, everything else Jesus did and said, including His coming to earth, the miracles He performed, and His teachings, would have been futile. We would still be in sin with no way out. Simply put, this one act of sacrifice by Jesus literally saved our lives, now and for all eternity. Jesus is the true picture of the Passover for us. The Passover lamb of the Old Testament symbolizes God's love for His people at that time; Jesus, Our Passover Lamb, symbolizes God's love for us today.

There is nothing more on God's part that can be done as far as our salvation is concerned. It is all up to us.

If we choose to ignore Jesus and His act of love, then we are saying to God and the world that we want to continue to live in sin and, in fact, enjoy the fruits that sin brings into our lives.

This is true for the church as well. We must fight the urge to be politically correct as opposed to biblically correct. It is critical that we replace sin in our lives as well as in the church with the forgiveness that accepting the blood of Jesus provides to both.

When Paul talks about leaven, he is drawing a picture that all those listening would have been familiar with. When leaven is put into dough and left in a warm place, the bread starts to rise, and at the right time, it is placed into the oven to stop the bread from growing.

If it were not stopped, it would continue to grow to the point that the whole batch would need to be thrown out. That is exactly what happens to us when sin is not dealt with in our lives. What started as a little sin will blow up and destroy our lives, homes, business, and churches. Sin has to be dealt with, and that is exactly what Jesus did when He died on the cross for us. He became Our Passover Lamb.

NAMES OF JESUS: P

Perfect Leader

God, for whom and through whom everything was made, chose to bring many children into glory. And it was only right that he should make Jesus, through his suffering, a perfect leader, fit to bring them into their salvation (Hebrews 2:10 NLT).

Jesus is our Perfect Leader in that He was the perfect sacrifice for our sins. Regardless of the suffering or trials or accusations made against Him, He remained Perfect. Jesus was and is the Perfect Leader for us.

Jesus' death on the cross was perfect in that He perfectly obeyed His Father. Whatever God does or directs to be done is perfect, and Jesus dying on the cross is no exception.

Jesus' Word is perfect. Whatever He promises He provides. Whatever He has prophesied has and will come to pass. The Word of God has been tried and tested and has been proven true for thousands of years.

Jesus' will is perfect. What safer place to be than in the will of God. When we ask Him to show us His will, and He does, we find delight in doing it and obtaining perfect peace as His will is accomplished.

Jesus is Perfect in all aspects of His life. The goal of all who follow Him should be that of becoming perfect as He is Perfect.

When the Perfect One comes into our lives, He brings with Him, according to James 1:17, good and perfect gifts. Have you ever received a gift that was either too big or too small or would not fit in your lifestyle? That will never happen when Jesus gives a gift. His gift will be perfect in need and desire, and it will move us forward to be perfect as our Lord and Savior, Jesus Christ—the Perfect Leader.

• • • • •

Physician

But when he heard it, he said, They that are whole have no need of a physician, but they that are sick (Matthew 9:12 ASV).

In His own words, Jesus is telling us that He has the prescription for our sin-sick souls. Jesus is concerned about giving us complete restoration. He is concerned about our physical, mental, financial, and spiritual ailments. Jesus has the prescription for all our needs. Are you heartbroken or suffering from loneliness? Is your home being torn apart? Has some type of addiction taken control of your life? Has some horrible news been delivered? Are you facing some disease that is life threatening? Well, great news! Jesus is a healing specialist in all these fields and any other situation that may arise in your life. Just as a doctor here on earth can only help those who call on him, Jesus can only minister to those who come to Him and allow Him to enter into their lives.

Sin is only fatal if we choose to let it be. No one needs to die from it. Jesus has provided the cure. How ridiculous to have a fatal disease like sin that can be cured but not make any attempt to be healed. A lot of people are carrying this sin disease because they choose to ignore it, are keeping it healthy by feeding it, or are just plain denying it.

Jesus has power over all the problems that we can ever have or imagine. Just think of being able to go to a doctor who has proven he has the ability to heal any disease or problem you now have or may develop in the future regardless of what it is. Another great thing about this doctor is that no appointment is necessary. Anytime, day or night, twenty-four hours a day, seven days a week, we can talk directly to the doctor Himself. To prove His sincerity for us to receive His counsel and obtain positive results, it costs us nothing. In fact, this Physician, Jesus, has already paid the bill in full.

This Physician, Jesus, was made available to us out of sincere love, and we must accept Him the exact same way.

Pleasing Aroma to God

Live a life filled with love, following the example of Christ. He loved us and offered himself as a sacrifice for us, a pleasing aroma to God (Ephesians 5:2 NLT).

Have you ever thought of Jesus as being a pleasing aroma? It sounds strange at first, yet many things about Him, including His teachings, sound strange to carnal ears. If we take a few minutes to examine this verse, we too will not only think of Jesus as a pleasing aroma but will thank Him for being so.

When the smoke of the sacrifice that Noah offered reached heaven, we are told that "The Lord smelled a sweet savour" (Genesis 8:21, KJV). In other words, God accepted it as a sacrifice.

When Jesus sacrificed Himself for our sins, the sacrifice

was acceptable to God. The sacrifice that Jesus offered was one of love. God did accept Jesus as a sacrifice, which enables us believers to be acceptable to God.

God is not obligated to receive any offering from us, regardless of size or amount of time we spend in preparing it for Him. God looks at the attitude as well as the intent of the giver.

Because of Jesus' sacrifice and God's willingness to accept it, we who accept Jesus into our lives become acceptable to God.

Jesus told His disciples to love one another as He had loved them. Because of this, we should love one another with a self-sacrificial love that is pleasing to Him.

God referred to many sacrifices as a pleasing aroma to Him. But none was more pleasing, beautiful, or satisfying than His One and Only Son, the Lord Jesus Christ.

If we need to be reminded of what real sacrifice and obedience are, all we have to do is look at Jesus, our sacrifice and Pleasing Aroma to God, our Father.

Pure

And everyone who really believes this will try to stay pure because Christ is pure (1 John 3:3 TLB).

God wants us to be just like His Son, Jesus. One of the motives for God's great love for us is purity. While we will never be one hundred percent pure until Jesus returns, we can certainly strive to obtain it.

Jesus is our purifier in the same sense that a metallurgist is a purifier of precious metals who works to remove impurities from these metals to make them as pure as possible. Just as the metals can't separate themselves from their impurities, we can't separate ourselves from our sins. We need someone to watch over and direct us away from sin and the things that make us impure.

When we start the purification process with Jesus, it is an ongoing one and will not be completed until we meet Jesus face to face.

What is really exciting about this process is that the purer we become, the purer we want to become.

There is much pleasure to be found as we start to know we are being cleansed. Many little things that we have accepted or participated in suddenly become unacceptable to us, like off-color jokes that we used to tell and thought of as only humor. However, as we grow in our purification process, we find these things really aren't funny anymore. Perhaps we would substitute words when we were angry for words that the world would use; however, we knew what we really wanted to say. Sadly, so did Jesus. I would add a word of caution here. The fact that we are being purified and growing does not qualify us as judge or jury. We must remember that we are all moving in the same direction and for the same reason, eternity with Jesus.

Even more than that, the Bible tells us that the Holy Spirit will be our guide, and no one is better qualified to lead us to the Pure One, the Lord Jesus Christ.

NAMES OF JESUS: R

Reality yet to Come

For these rules are only shadows of the reality yet to come. And Christ himself is that reality (Colossians 2:17 NLT).

When Jesus comes into our lives, we realize that nothing else can or will satisfy like the Holy Spirit living in our hearts. That, my friend, is reality; no rule or ritual can take the place of the living God we serve. The reality is that Jesus speaks, hears, acts, sees, and thinks. No ritual can do this, and no rule is able to do anything other than surrender to humankind's interpretation.

Rules and rituals have no life. Even though they may point us toward Jesus, they have no sustainable life within them.

A dream exists and functions only in the mind of the dreamer. We fall short when we try approaching God with claims of having good ethics and morals or claims of giving to and serving the church.

The true approach to God is Jesus. Jesus was and is perfect, and He stands as the true reality of God. Jesus is the only way to come into the presence of God. God only accepts those who come to Him through Jesus. There is no other way to please God than being obedient to Jesus and His teachings.

If it is our desire to live in the reality of Jesus, we must remember that when someone decides to follow Jesus, that person has to make a conscientious decision to live as Jesus lived. We must set examples for others by the habits and desires we pursue, the places we frequent, as well as the conversations that fill our lives. We should worship as Jesus worshiped, by following the teachings of the Holy Word of God. The list of what it means to live in the reality of Jesus could go on and on.

One encouraging thing about following Jesus is that He is with us, knowing that we will make mistakes, stumble, and oftentimes fall. The real and true reality is that Jesus will pick us up, brush us off, grab hold of our hands, and continue leading us to His Father, God.

• • • • •

Redeemer

For I know that my redeemer liveth, and that he shall stand at the latter day upon the earth (Job 19:25 KJV).

Throughout the Bible, we find the words *redeem* and *redeemer*. To redeem is to purchase or buy something. The person purchasing or buying something would be the redeemer. When we look, however, at Jesus, our Redeemer, we are not talking about redeeming some material object that is temporal, but we are talking about redeeming our souls, which will never die.

What makes Jesus our perfect Redeemer? For one thing, Jesus took on the form of man and became flesh and blood in order to be related to us through His blood, thereby making us joint heirs to His throne. He became willing to the point that His mind was set on the cross. He made this decision before He ever left His Father's side in heaven. We should never forget that our Redeemer is living and continues to redeem us from death by interceding on our behalf and by having the precious Holy Spirit continue in our lives.

How blessed we are to be able to have a personal relationship with not only the living Son of God but also with our Redeemer as well. When we examine Jesus, our Redeemer, just the fact that He died for us should be enough for us to praise Him from now until He calls us home.

When He became our Redeemer, He redeemed us from confusion and chaos to rest and peace, from worry and fear to security and confidence, from sorrow and hatred to joy and love, from uncertainty and pain to faithfulness and provision, from sin and eternal death to salvation and eternal life.

Jesus not only redeemed us from all evil and the debt owed for sin, but He also made payment in full and canceled the debt for all eternity. That is why Jesus is our Redeemer.

Resurrection and the Life

> *Jesus told her, "I am the resurrection and the life. Anyone who believes in me will live, even after dying"* (John 11:25 NLT).

If any Scripture was ever written that was worthy of not only being quoted but also remembered throughout the days of our lives, this is it.

What other statement could Jesus make that would so clearly establish His identity as being one of supreme divinity?

Notice that Jesus didn't say He would give us the resurrection or that He would give life to us. He very clearly states that He is the Resurrection and He is the Life. This statement further implies that Jesus is not only the power and the source of life but the very beginning and being of it. This claim clearly establishes that not only does Jesus resurrect and give life, but He sustains and restores it as well.

One reason Jesus can make this dynamic claim is that the power He has comes from the fact that He is the Creator of life. It only stands to reason that since He created life, it would be a simple task for Him to restore it. In John 14:19, we find a supportive statement in that Jesus says, "Because I live, you also will live" (NRSV). Knowing Jesus and His power and knowing that He is leading and directing our lives through the Holy Spirit should tell us how wonderful Jesus is. If we maintain our faith and confidence in Jesus and His living Word, we can enjoy communication with Him and be in constant fellowship with Him, knowing in time we will spend eternity with both those who have gone on before us and with Jesus, our Resurrection and Life.

• • • • •

Righteousness

And this will be his name: "The LORD Is Our Righteousness." In that day Judah will be saved, and Israel will live in safety (Jeremiah 23:6 NLT).

We find this claim being reinforced in 1 John 2:1 where it says, "Jesus Christ, the Righteous One" (NIV). How is Jesus Our Righteousness? One way is that the plan for our salvation began with Jesus. Not only that, Jesus secured Our Righteousness, and through His continuing to be our Advocate, we continue to receive righteousness.

Because Jesus' righteousness opposes humankind's sinfulness, it gives us hope when we feel condemnation or guilt for our sins. Those of us who have committed our lives to Jesus will not be punished because Jesus has paid the price and taken our punishment upon Himself. Jesus took on the sins of the world for believers and unbelievers alike. What category we fit into is our decision.

Because of Jesus' righteousness, God hears and answers our prayers and forgives us of our sins. God will accept nothing else on our behalf. There is no other righteousness or goodness that God has approved to be righteous enough to enter His presence for the benefit of humankind.

If we stood alone before God, we would have to argue our own reputations and works and that we had done the best we could.

Jesus pleads the one thing that humankind does not have, and that is His own righteousness

In order to grow and maintain Our Righteousness, we need to maintain and grow our faith. It is through faith that a real connection with Jesus takes root. When faith starts its growth, love and obedience grow with it.

Righteousness will then gain a foothold, and our prayer will, without a doubt, be, "Jesus, please be our Righteousness now and forever."

● ● ● ● ●

The Rose of Sharon

I am the rose of Sharon, and the lily of the valleys (Song of Songs 2:1 KJV).

We will be hard-pressed to find a more descriptive illustration of our Lord than that of the Rose of Sharon.

When we think of the rose, we think of a flower God made that, when compared to all others in totality, is the loveliest and the sweetest. It has three perfect features: shape, color, and fragrance. Some have gone as far as to call the rose the queen of flowers.

When we call Jesus the Rose of Sharon, we won't find Him in the rich soil of the garden beds or the soil of the mountains or valleys. This Rose grows and blooms in the soil of human hearts. This growth can be found in young as well as old hearts. He grows just as well in the rich as He does in the poor. This flower can be found growing in all the hearts of all the nations throughout the world. What a beautiful flower is this Rose of Sharon! Regardless of where we search, we will find none other like Him in all the earth.

The Rose of Sharon has many uses, and they are all for our benefit. Not only is the Rose of Sharon beautiful in appearance to us now, but He will be the most beautiful sight in all of heaven. The Rose of Sharon has a lovely fragrance for us just as He did when God accepted Him as a pleasing aroma for us sinners. The Rose of Sharon bears fruit in that we who taste see how good and pleasant it is for our souls. The Rose of Sharon never fades, nor does His beauty ever diminish. He replaces hurt and sorrow with joy when nothing else can because His beauty is ever increasing.

How blessed we are to have as the centerpiece of our lives the Rose of Sharon!

NAMES OF JESUS: S

Savior

For unto you is born this day in the city of David a Saviour, which is Christ the Lord (Luke 2:11 KJV).

We read and hear this Scripture so much at Christmastime that it has perhaps lost its real meaning and the impact it should have on such a sinful world. As our Savior, Jesus has delivered us from the power of sin as well as its penalty. We have been delivered from both death and judgment.

Our world is in desperate need of a savior. The sin and lack of morals that exist in this world are destroying lives and homes at a pace that the world has never experienced. While the world tries to provide itself with a savior, it is only temporary at best, and any savior that the world tries to provide proves to have feet of clay, a heart of ice, and a mind of self-service.

Jesus our Savior is sent directly from God and is God. Although He is the Savior of the world, this truth does not mean that the world will be saved.

If you are drowning and someone throws you a lifeline, you still have to make the decision to reach out and take hold or let go and drown. The decision is yours.

Jesus is the only One with the knowledge and power to save humankind from themselves, from the world of sin, and from all the evil effects that sin has brought into it. He also sits at the right hand of God the Father in all His glory. He alone has power and dominion over the heavens and earth and all created things.

Knowing this brings us to one simple act, and that is to ask

Jesus to be our Savior and praise Him for all He has done, is doing, and will continue to do, now and for all eternity.

• • • • •

The Savior of All Men

For therefore we both labour and suffer reproach, because we trust in the living God, who is the Saviour of all men, specially of those that believe (1 Timothy 4:10 KJV).

Wow! Jesus is not the Savior of just the wealthy, or the highly educated, or a select race, but He is the Savior of all who choose to serve Him.

Jesus saves us from all the consequences of sin as well as from sin itself. Jesus dying on the cross covered all of humankind's sins. This does not mean, however, that salvation or the forgiveness of our sins is automatic. Jesus forces Himself upon no one. To obtain this free gift of salvation, we have to ask Jesus for forgiveness of the sin in our lives and commit to live for Him according to His will and His Word. If we trust in Him, His promises of eternal life with Him will be ours. If not, His promises of eternal separation from Him will be ours. The choice is up to us.

His salvation brings many blessings with it, such as strength, joy, protection, security, and light in the dark, just to name a few.

In order to have a perfect Savior, we need to have one who is not only willing but also able. I am sure there are many who would be willing to be a savior, but only Jesus has the ability. We can ask others, and, in fact, in some circles, people pronounce their forgiveness of our sins. How foolish. If humankind could forgive humankind, there would be no need for Jesus. If we had no need for Jesus, then why would we need His precious Holy Spirit? And if we need neither, then we have no need for God. What a lie Satan has sold to humankind.

How blessed we are to have a Savior who is interested in every moment of our lives and is willing to be involved in our lives as deliver, healer, rescuer, protector, and provider of all our needs.

Truly, we are blessed by Jesus, the Savior of All Men.

• • • • •

Slave

Instead, he gave up his divine privileges; he took the humble position of a slave and was born as a human being. When he appeared in human form (Philippians 2:7 NLT).

Why would one who is called King of kings, Son of God, and many more illustrious names choose to be called Slave? Only one word comes to mind, and that is love.

Out of love, the One we should be slaves to came and became a slave for us. The One whom we should minister to chose to minister to us. The One we should search for came and searched for and continues to search for us.

Jesus could have come with such armies that humankind, out of fear for their lives, would have surrendered to Him immediately. Instead He came with such meekness that humankind bullied Him. Instead of surrendering to Him, they took Him captive and killed Him. People to this day still look and are impressed by what is on the outside, never seeing or enjoying what is on the inside.

We would be wise to remember that while Jesus became a slave, He did so knowing we needed Him to serve us. He does not need us to serve Him. He wants us to, but He is Perfect and the Son of God regardless of what we do. We are the ones who change because of this Slave. He never changes anything because of us. This is why we should serve Him out of love like little children, not out of fear that He might in some way harm us.

We should want to become slaves like Jesus. Our first duty should be to willingly serve His Father as He did. We are allowed to be joint heirs to the kingdom of God all because of Jesus, a Slave.

Someone Who Is Alive

The women were terrified and bowed with their faces to the ground. Then the men asked, "Why are you looking among the dead for someone who is alive?" (Luke 24:5 NLT)

Where do we look for Jesus? is an interesting question, not just to be asked then but to be asked today.

What were these women carrying to the tomb of Jesus? They were carrying the embalming materials of that day, the most precious and valuable spices as well as the finest white linen. What was their intent? It was to embalm Jesus. They were going to honor a dead Man, one who was powerless to help them any longer, let alone help them through all eternity. All of the women's actions, conversations, and goals were focused on a dead Man. The women may not have been aware of it, but they were confirming what the world had declared. Jesus was just another man whom death had added to its list of victims. When we are posed with the question of where we look for Jesus, what is our answer?

When we first hear of Jesus being resurrected, we often need time to try and comprehend such a story. We may perceive it to be a fairy tale and hard to believe. Even when we check out the facts about what happened, we are still confused.

It is only when we have a personal encounter with Jesus that we start to accept the validity of the resurrection. As we start to spend time studying the Word of God, praying, getting acquainted with the precious Holy Spirit, and serving God, the understanding of reality starts to become clear.

We only find Jesus when we look for Him in the right places. He will not be found in bad habits, in corruption, or in bad words, thoughts, or actions. We will, however, find the One Who Is Alive when we pattern our lives after His. We truly become alive because we find Jesus, the One Who Is Alive.

• • • • •

Son of the Living God

And Simon Peter answered and said, Thou art the Christ, the Son of the living God (Matthew 16:16 KJV).

Christ is God's only begotten Son. He is not adopted. He is not an angel or some other being promoted to this high level. He is the true living Son of God. Jesus is alive physically, spiritually, and mentally. All of this is extremely important in our lives.

That we serve a living God who has a living Son who intercedes for us as well as a living Holy Spirit to help and guide us is significant. The reference to God living is also found in the Old Testament in 2 Kings 19:16.

We serve a living God as opposed to a lifeless piece of wood or concrete that has ears but cannot hear, eyes but cannot see, lips but cannot speak, and that depends on a person to take it from place to place as well as provide for its upkeep. Our living God sees, hears, speaks, thinks, and provides for us. We also depend on God for our spiritual upkeep. The life that is in our living God is also in us. We are able to communicate with our living God anytime, anyplace, or anywhere. When was the last time you talked to a piece of wood or concrete, regardless of the image, and it spoke back?

It took the disciples a long time to come to the point in their lives where they could confess the fact that Jesus was the Son of the Living God. They had to deal with the bitter resentments of the Jewish religious leaders. Some of their friends and family rejected them. Then, of course, they had to deal with their own personal inner conflict over who Jesus really was. When they really examined the facts, they came to the realization that Jesus was their only real hope. He was the only source for salvation as well as the only Savior for all humankind.

We too will come to the same understanding when we take the time to get to know Jesus, the Son of the Living God.

• • • • •

Source of Eternal Salvation

In this way, God qualified him as a perfect High Priest, and he became the source of eternal salvation for all those who obey him (Hebrews 5:9 NLT).

What is salvation? We are told that Jesus provides it for us and that God offers it to us. In all messages, we are told that we should want it, so what is it? Well, put simply, *salvation* means being saved from God's judgment. It creates in us joy and peace; it lets us start and end each day knowing that Jesus loves us and wants to be a part of our lives every day.

If we have or want to have salvation, there has to be a source, a place where we can go and get it. There has to be a reason for wanting it, and there has to be an assurance that it is genuine and eternally lasting.

We notice first in this verse that Jesus is the appointed source for salvation, and this is not a self-appointed responsibility. It is an appointment made by God. We also notice that it is for all eternity if (perhaps the biggest if we will ever deal with) we obey Jesus.

If we are going to learn obedience to Jesus, we first have to believe that Jesus is who He says He is and then believe His teachings. By nature, we desire to live the way we want rather than the way Jesus says we should. But if we truly believe Jesus, then we will obey His Word because we do believe Him.

If we look back at the verse in Hebrews, it is very clear that Jesus, the Source of Eternal Salvation, is for all who obey Him. Simply, it is our decision and ours alone—to obey Jesus or not.

Source of Peace

And he will be the source of peace. When the Assyrians invade our land and break through our defenses, we will appoint seven rulers to watch over us, eight princes to lead us (Micah 5:5 NLT).

World leaders plan and strategize, call for summits, and write treaties. Some even go so far as to threaten military action in order to obtain peace.

People themselves spend untold millions of dollars searching for peace. Here, in this Scripture, is not only peace but the very Source of Peace.

Some try to find peace by moving to a new location. They change jobs or spouses in an attempt to avoid the problems that they perceive are causing them unrest. Jesus' solution is for us to hold His hand and through prayer and faith conquer the problem. In the world, peace often lasts only as long as our money.

The peace that Jesus gives passes all human understanding, will withstand any attack, and will be with us as long as we hold onto Jesus. The peace that is obtained in the world is changeable and can be lost. The peace that Jesus offers is from an unchanging God.

Does it make sense to have peace when we are going through family problems, have just been advised that some horrific disease is attacking our body, or have just lost a loved one? While we may experience the natural emotions, beneath all of that is a peace that tells us God is with us. This is not some self-induced feeling. It is a gift that is given to those who follow Jesus because of the love God has for us.

The peace that Jesus gives far surpasses positive thinking or just claiming that there really is no problem. It is more than just a warm, fuzzy feeling. It is not brought about by changing our attitudes. It is the peace of God.

It does not depend upon our conditions or our surroundings, and nothing, absolutely nothing, can rob us of it. It is the peace that comes from Jesus, the Source of Peace.

• • • • •

Stone That Makes People Stumble

And, "He is the stone that makes people stumble, the rock that makes them fall." They stumble because they do not obey God's word, and so they meet the fate that was planned for them (1 Peter 2:8 NLT).

The first thought that comes to mind is why Jesus would want people to stumble. The obvious answer is He doesn't, but because of their decisions, that is exactly what happens.

Jesus was the cause of the Jews' stumbling when He was here on earth because He didn't come with all the glamour and pomp that they expected. After all, He was born in poor surroundings; His family was poor, and then He grew up to associate with non-Jews. In addition, He challenged the Jews' views on the law as well as the Scriptures.

People look at Jesus and stumble because they want complete knowledge and understanding of Him before they are willing to have faith in Him. Understanding how Jesus could be anything other than just a common man like the rest of us is difficult for the carnal mind. When it comes to Jesus' death, we question how it could be anything more than the death of another martyr who was fighting for a cause. The very idea of someone being resurrected could be nothing more than a well-orchestrated tale made up by His followers.

Many people just do not believe in Jesus as the Son of God; therefore, they have trouble understanding that God sent Him into the world for our benefit.

The gut-wrenching truth is that God is not affected by what we say or think about Him. However, our present lives as well as our eternal lives are affected by what He thinks of us. Come judgment day, it will be too late to beg for forgiveness or tell Him how wrong and sorry we are.

While Jesus is the Stone That Makes People Stumble, He is also the One who tells us that our feet will never stumble if we will walk with our hands in His hand. So whether we walk upright or stumble, the choice is clearly ours.

• • • • •

Supreme over All Creation

> *Christ is the visible image of the invisible God. He existed before anything was created and is supreme over all creation* (Colossians 1:15 NLT).

Doesn't this title just quicken your spirit? Jesus is the firstborn of all creation, and He came from heaven. Remember, He created the dust; He was not created from it.

Jesus' supremacy over all creation would, of course, include the spirit world. We need to be cautious not to lose sight of the deity of Jesus, meaning that He is God. Popular teachings and words being coined can vary subtly and cause us to move off center of the truth of Jesus' teachings. We are told that we need to be politically correct or be sensitive to others' feelings. By all means, we should learn from others, respect other cultures, love and pray for all people of the world, ask God to meet their needs, fill them with His love and peace, forgive them of their sins, and use them in spreading His Word. But in doing so, we should not compromise the message that Jesus is both man and God. He created the heavens and the earth and is Lord of lords and King of kings. He rules over all powers, good and bad, and has dominion over death and hell. Perhaps the greatest point of non-compromise is that Jesus died for our sins, arose victorious over sin and death, and now sits at the right hand of God the Father.

This supremacy was given to Jesus by God. God exalted Jesus above all creatures, not only in our world today but in the world to come. No one else sits beside God except Jesus. God exalted Him above "all principality, and power, and might, and dominion" (Ephesians 1:21, KJV). Then God made sure that there would be no confusion about His intent. He exalted Jesus above "every name that is named, not only in this world, but also in that which is to come" (Ephesians 1:21, KJV).

What great news for those of us who are followers of Jesus. Thank God, He is not only supreme over our lives; He is Supreme over All Creation.

NAMES OF JESUS: T

Tabernacle of God

And I heard a great voice out of heaven saying, Behold, the tabernacle of God is with men, and he will dwell with them, and they shall be his people, and God himself shall be with them, and be their God (Revelation 21:3 KJV).

We are all aware that the Bible holds many great truths. Its stories lift our hearts to new heights as well as bring us to tears. There are verses that most of the world could quote. Names written within are used or referred to almost daily. Still I find no greater promise and description of Jesus written between the covers of this great book, the Bible, than that of the Tabernacle of God.

When God created humankind, nothing separated humankind from God's presence. Then Adam and Eve sinned and disobeyed God. At that instant, everything changed. The door was shut and shut tight. No longer would humankind be allowed in God's presence.

However, God's love for humankind never stopped, and His plan for redemption was put into place. Part of the beginning of His plan included the Tabernacle. God gave Moses the exact measurements, blueprints, and details for the Tabernacle including the furnishings and how it was to function. Humankind knew exactly what God expected from them as well as what they could expect from Him.

Jesus is now the Tabernacle for humankind. The only way to have fellowship with God is to recognize that we need atonement for our sins, and that requires Jesus' sacrificial blood.

Many teach and would like to believe that there are many ways to approach God, but humankind can be saved and enter into the presence of God only one way, and that is through Jesus. He allows humankind access to God anytime, anyplace.

Jesus is, in fact, all and more than the Tabernacle. When we look at the Brazen Altar and think of all the sacrifices that took place day after day, year after year, we see a picture of Calvary. When we see the Laver, we see the picture of Jesus washing away our sins. When we see the Table of Shewbread, we see a picture of Jesus as the Bread of Life, always in the presence of God. We think of the Altar of Incense as a picture of humankind's prayers and praise going up to Jesus, our Intercessor, and as a symbol of His continuing ministry.

Jesus truly is the Tabernacle of God and much, so much, more.

• • • • •

Tried Stone

Therefore thus saith the Lord God, Behold, I lay in Zion for a foundation a stone, a tried stone, a precious corner stone, a sure foundation: he that believeth shall not make haste (Isaiah 28:16 KJV).

As a Tried Stone, Jesus was qualified to answer all the questions for which He came.

Jesus was tried in ways we will never experience. He was tried in obedience from birth to death. His meekness was tried by both verbal and physical abuse. His patience was tried every step of the way to the cross. His innocence was tried as well as

His temper. His love for all humankind was tried every day of His ministry. Jesus was tried by His enemies as well as His friends. In both cases, He responded with the same attitude. As our Savior, He continues to be tried by us daily. His mercy and His willingness to hear and answer our prayers continue today to be tried.

When we commit to following Jesus, He, in turn, tries us. He tries our hearts to be sure we are fully committed to serving Him. He wants to be assured that our obedience and desires are directed to Him and not ourselves.

He tries us to be sure that we complete the goal He has set before us. As people watched to see if Jesus failed, He is aware that people are watching us for the same reason.

Jesus has been tried by time through corruption in society and in churches, yet He stands victorious over all.

Truly, Jesus is a Tried Stone, tried and proven to be the same yesterday, today, and forever.

True Vine

"I am the true vine, and my Father is the husbandman" (John 15:1 KJV).

Jesus is saying to us that as the True Vine, He is our source of everything that is good in our lives. This comparison calls to our attention the fact that the vine feeds the branches. Through Jesus, we get the strength, direction, and purpose He has for our lives. Through this True Vine, Jesus, we fulfill His plan for our lives. I like the way the New Living Translation Bible puts it, "I am the true grapevine, and my Father is the gardener." Successful gardeners know how to produce the best crops as well as how to care for them. This involves cutting off branches that don't bear fruit or cutting back some of the branches, even though this may hurt for a brief time. When the branches grow back, they are stronger and produce strong, healthy fruit. Often, some branches are cut from the vine because they continually draw from the vine and use up its life-giving nutrients while refusing to be productive. When these branches are cut from the vine, this allows life-giving nutrients to be given to the other branches, so they can continue to produce strong and healthy fruit.

As a gardener, God has planted Jesus in our midst. Jesus tells us in John 15:6 what happens to the branches that leave Him and go off on their own in an effort to produce their own fruit

We make choices every day that have an effect upon our life, now as well as in the future. No choice is more important than the one we make when we choose which vine we will attach our lives to. The vine of the world will lead us into evil and ungodliness and eventually a life and eternity with Satan.

The other vine, the True Vine, will lead us into the world of righteousness and grace and eventually a life and eternity with Jesus.

The Truth

Jesus told him, "I am the way, the truth, and the life. No one can come to the Father except through me" (John 14:6 NLT).

Jesus is the Truth; He is not a form, type, or reflection of truth but is the actual source from which all truth comes. It makes absolutely no difference what orders He gives, what statement He makes, or what answer He gives to any question He is asked, it is the Truth. There is not the slightest hint or shadow of dishonesty in Jesus.

There is a vast difference between telling someone what truth is and actually living the Truth. Jesus was a complete picture of Truth. He not only spoke the Truth, but He lived and died for it, arose from the grave embracing it, and went to sit at His Father's right hand to see it fully manifested in the lives of those for whom He died.

We hear a lot about the freedom to express ourselves; however, Jesus didn't suffer and die so we can express ourselves and do our own thing. In reality, His death delivered us from doing our own thing and should instill in us a desire to do His thing, which is spreading the Truth of His Gospel. That Gospel is more than just learning the Truth of Jesus; it is living the Truth of Jesus. His Truth is something that settles deep down in our soul and demands to be cared for and fed on a regular basis.

The Truth is always at peace in the presence of its Father. One of the most important things about the Truth is that every promise Jesus spoke in His Word is true. When He says He will forgive our sins, it is the Truth. When He says we can spend all eternity with Him, it is the Truth. When He says He will supply all our needs, it is the Truth. When He says He will heal our bodies, it is the Truth. When Jesus says He will never leave us nor forsake us and will stick by us closer than a brother, it is the Truth.

Life will never be lived or enjoyed the way the Creator meant for it to be until we accept Jesus as Lord and Master of our lives, and that is the Truth.

* * * * *

The Veil

By a new and living way, which he hath consecrated for us, through the veil, that is to say, his flesh (Hebrews 10:20 KJV).

This name, at first, seems to be unusual, but it doesn't take long before we realize what a beautiful name it really is.

When we think of a veil, we generally think of something that provides access to something or someone. This is exactly what our Veil, Jesus, did. He provided access to God. This was something that had never been available before. Our Veil opened up a close and personal relationship with God for us. Because of our Veil, we have the ability to enter into God's presence anytime, and if our relationship is such, God has the ability to talk with us anytime He chooses.

When our Veil, Jesus, died on the cross, the veil in the temple was destroyed. However, our Veil arose, giving us a new way of accessing God. We need not only understand but also live in our relationship with God with the knowledge that because of Jesus we are as close to God as He is.

We have been given the ability to enter into God's presence

with boldness. We might think we have this boldness because we are counted as brothers and sisters with Jesus. Actually, we are given this boldness because our Veil is now restored, whereas the old veil remains destroyed and will never be restored to its former place.

We now have great and precious promises given to us by God through His Son, Jesus. Every day of our lives, every waking moment, we have not only the promises of God but also the precious blood of Jesus that covers all. We also have the precious, loving, caring, and supporting Holy Spirit. We have all of this because of our Veil, the Lord Jesus Christ.

The Visible Image of the Invisible God

Christ is the visible image of the invisible God. He existed before anything was created and is supreme over all creation (Colossians 1:15 NLT).

First Timothy 6:16 (NLT) reads in part, "No human eye has ever seen him, nor ever will." These words, however, do not mean we have not seen the exact image of God. This verse should not be interpreted to mean that Jesus is a copy of God. Rather, it means that Jesus is the perfect representation of God.

When Jesus walked upon this earth, humankind was able to see how loving, caring, concerned, just, and holy He is. Righteousness was evident everywhere He went. His compassion for people was seen in His many miracles of healing and restoration of minds as well as bodies. Jesus gave His all that humankind might be saved. These and many more attributes let us see exactly what God is like. People can argue about the color of Jesus' eyes, hair, skin, and other physical characteristics, and the truth will go unanswered. The real truth is that these attributes do not matter as far as our salvation and eternity are concerned.

When Jesus came to earth, He came as God in flesh. He came to show us what God is like and His desire to fellowship with humankind. By walking among humankind, Jesus made it clear that God is near. He showed us that God cares. For example, just read all the miracles and promises that are recorded in His Holy Word. Remember, when Jesus died on the cross, He did so to show the love God has for us. Jesus could have called angels to stop what was happening at any time.

Jesus has always been the Image of God; this was not a new role. We serve an unchanging God, the same yesterday, today, and forever.

Before He came to earth, while He walked upon this earth, and now as He sits at the right hand of God the Father, Jesus continues to be the Image of God.

NAMES OF JESUS: W

The Way

> *Jesus told him, "I am the way, the truth, and the life. No one can come to the Father except through me"* (John 14:6 NLT).

How is Jesus the Way? Certainly, He is the Way in that He does not just point the way to salvation, but He takes us by the hand and leads us. He doesn't sit back and give us directions; He shows us He truly is the Way.

The fact that Jesus was both man and God gave Him great insight into what the needs and challenges in our lives would be.

Jesus is the Way that enables us to obtain directions and protection that we can depend upon and to grow in our relationship with Him. Jesus is the Way for us. He is our direct connection to God. We should obediently follow Him, trusting His guidance and ability to do for us what we could never do for ourselves.

Many desire to follow a path that leads them to a financially and personally successful career. Many follow a path that leads to intellectual achievement. But when it comes to following the way Jesus has established for them, they stumble. Some fall, and others retreat while never tasting the complete success that Jesus had planned for them.

We may have asked or been asked, "How do I get to heaven?" Jesus Himself answered that question with a direct answer, "I am the way." There is no other way for humankind to enter into the presence of God and spend all eternity with Him.

Notice, Jesus didn't say that church attendance is the way, although this is important for our spiritual growth. He didn't say giving to the church is the way, although this is something we will want to do once we get to know Jesus. He didn't say working in the church is the way, even though this could happen if we are obedient to Jesus.

Jesus made it clear that He is the Way, to follow His teachings, and to be obedient to His commands; then all the promises in God's Word will be ours. Jesus has told us that He is the Way to all God has to offer.

The Word

In the beginning the Word already existed. The Word was with God, and the Word was God (John 1:1 NLT).

Perhaps no other name describes Jesus as completely as does this name: from being with God in the beginning; to being born in the flesh on earth; to dying on the cross; to conquering sin and death; to ascending back to the Father; to returning to earth, rescuing His people, and destroying His enemies in a war such as humankind has never seen. The most amazing thing is that all of this did happen, is happening, and will happen by the Word.

The Word of God is so gentle that it can create life. It is so loving that it can forgive sin. It is so caring that it can heal bodies of all sickness and diseases. It is so final that those who disobey it will one day be removed forever from His presence.

In 1 John 1:1, Jesus is called the Word of Life. Not only did Jesus give physical life, but He also gives spiritual life. In Revelation 19:13, Jesus is called the Word of God. This verse shows that He is speaking for God and is, in fact, the final Word. Jesus is going to destroy all evil, filth, sin, and death on this earth.

Notice, the weapon He uses is so powerful that nothing now or anything developed in the future will be strong enough to defeat His weapon. Guess what? When we wage war against the trials, temptations, sickness, and worries that affect our daily lives, we already have this weapon in our spiritual arsenal. This weapon is called God's Word.

When we pause and reflect on creation, we can see how powerful His Word really is. He spoke, and the world, including all the planets, galaxies, sun, moon, and stars, came into being. He spoke, and all the vegetation, animal life, seas, oceans, rivers, lakes, mountains, and valleys came into being. He spoke, and humankind was made in His image.

God is no liar. What God says, He will do. After all, He gave us His Word.

Names of Jesus: Y

Your Example

For God called you to do good, even if it means suffering, just as Christ suffered for you. He is your example, and you must follow in his steps (1 Peter 2:21 NLT).

Jesus set many examples for His followers to follow. We will never suffer the way Jesus did. However, He showed us how to handle suffering when it comes our way.

Jesus is a great example of learning how to show gentleness, humility, perseverance, maturity, and grace. Followers of Jesus should have these attributes in their lives as the world observes their lifestyles.

It is never a good idea to try to be something we aren't. What we are should come naturally to us. What we really are, what we really think, and how we really act will always come out when things get tense or pressure is on us, and we lose our cool. You can paint a skunk the color of a rose, even go as far as to call it a rose, but under pressure, it is still going to stink.

Jesus never once wavered in His confidence that His Father, God, was always with Him, leading and guiding Him in a way that brought peace and direction. Jesus' every need was met. When He needed to feed a large number of people, the food was there by faith. When He needed to heal a damaged or diseased body, the miracle was there by faith. When He needed to fight off Satan in a face-to-face confrontation, the words were there by faith. When we need to depend on Jesus for any reason, He will be there by faith.

The real reason we need to be an example and follow after

Jesus is that's what He wants us to do. This is one way we can please Him. In Matthew 11:29 (TLB) we read, "Wear my yoke—for it fits perfectly—and let me teach you; for I am gentle and humble, and you shall find rest for your souls." This is Jesus telling us why He should be our Example.

• • • • •

Your Ransom

God chose him as your ransom long before the world began, but he has now revealed him to you in these last days (1 Peter 1:20 NLT).

This verse is perhaps one of the strongest pertaining to the fact that Jesus has always existed with God as well as the fact that He is all knowing. Here is a plan that was decided long before creation.

Since God and His judgment are eternal, our sins obviously require an eternal ransom. Jesus promises eternal life to all who believe in and on Him.

When something or someone is ransomed, something of value is exchanged for something else of value. When money is paid to a kidnapper, the person paying the money is showing that the family member or friend is of greater value than this money. The kidnapper is saying just the opposite; the money is worth more than this person's life.

The statement God made to the world through His Son, Jesus, is that humankind's souls are as precious to Him as His own Son. God, in His omniscience, knew no one or nothing else could be used and accepted except the perfect, sinless, and pure man, Your Ransom, Jesus. We must always remember that Jesus gave of Himself freely. In no way was Jesus forced onto the cross. He could have called angels from heaven at any time and stopped the crucifixion.

In Matthew 20:28, Jesus explains that He didn't come to be waited on but to serve others and to be sacrificed as a ransom for many. Jesus died for the entire world. The sad part is that not all the world wants to be ransomed.

We can embrace many theories, philosophies, or religions. But the reality of life is that there is only one God and only one Mediator. He is Our Ransom, Jesus.

After Jesus went to be with His Father, He left the precious gift of the Holy Spirit to do many works in your life. One is to help us understand why God's Son, the Lord Jesus Christ, became Your Ransom.

Conclusion

Perhaps the greatest blessing of all is that we have the choice to serve God or not. We have just read one hundred and one reasons to serve Him and there are many more.

When we serve Him, we need to apply the power that comes with knowing Him not only to our everyday life but to the trials, tribulations, and the spiritual attacks that we have been told from the Word of God will come our way.

> *For we wrestle not against flesh and blood, but against principalities, against powers, against the rulers of the darkness of this world, against spiritual wickedness in high places* (Ephesians 6:12 KJV) .

When this happens, the power that we possess because of Jesus makes us more than conquerers through Him. Victory is assured; peace surrounds us as well as lives in us. Our mind starts to focus on the work He has given us, and we become confident that with His help we will accomplish the goals He has set before us.

When it comes to provisions, we have the Source of all creation looking out for us. The provisions that God has for us started at Calvary and will continue on through eternity. God has provided for the forgiveness of our sins, a life of peace while living here on earth, and an eternity with our loved ones who have chosen to serve Him, as well as sharing all eternity with Jesus, Himself. In further detail, He provides us with healing, forgiveness, light, faith, laughter, purpose, work, hope, rest, food, wisdom, shelter, strength, friends, and family. Because He is full of infinite grace, His blessings never end.

Truly we are a blessed people who have been allowed the privilege of not only speaking the name of Jesus but expecting and receiving power and provisions through the names of Jesus.

> *And whatsoever ye shall ask in my name, that will I do, that the Father may be glorified in the Son* (John 14:13 KJV).

About the Author

DANIEL GUBITZ has been a businessman and entrepreneur for more than fifty years. He started out as a bellman in a small motel and worked his way up to become area manager for one of the largest motel chains in the industry.

He and his wife, LaDonna, have owned and operated child development centers for the past forty years as well. During that time they have had more than thirty-five foster children in their home. For more than forty years, Daniel has counselled in all types of family situations. He has spent more than twenty-five years in Christian ministry, from starting new works to serving in established churches. He and his wife have enjoyed fifty years of marriage.

He may be contacted by e-mail at: dltal@mauigateway.com